MGB
OWNER'S
SURVIVAL
MANUAL

CLASSIC
CARS

MGB
OWNER'S
SURVIVAL
MANUAL

JIM TYLER

ACKNOWLEDGEMENTS

Friends and family for their encouragement. Neighbours for their tolerance. Em, Dave and Chalkie for an education in car repair and restoration. Osprey for publishing the book. Canon, Yashica and Zenith for making cameras tough enough to withstand life in my workshop.

For this book I did all of the work on my car myself, giving me the advantage of being able to write from first-hand experience. I took the photographs of myself work-ing on the car using the shutter time delay on my cameras. To anyone who expects to see photographs depicting professional mechanics in spotlessly clean overalls (and with clean fingernails) pretending to work on a car, instead of a scruffy middle-aged fool with grease, dirt and (often) blood on his hands, I can only offer my apologies.

I'm 41 years of age (dammit), and live in rural Worcestershire in England with my wife, two dogs, a '66 MGB GT, '74 Midget, '68 Morris Minor and a '70 VW Beetle for winter use.

First published in Great Britain in 1995
by Osprey, an imprint of Reed Consumer Books Limited,
Michelin House, 81 Fulham Road, London SW3 6RB
and Auckland, Melbourne, Singapore and Toronto.

ISBN 1 85532 493 8

Editor Shaun Barrington
Designed by Design Revolution

Printed in Italy by G. Canale & C. S.p.A. - Borgaro T.se - TURIN

For a catalogue of all books published by Osprey Automotive
please write to:
The Marketing Department, Reed Consumer Books,
1st Floor, Michelin House, 81 Fulham Road, London SW3 6RB

Contents

Introduction

t's a sportscar. It's comfortable. It's reliable. It's fun to drive. It's got more character about it than any modern car – including the latest 'Classic British sportscar' lookalike from the Far East. It's over thirty years old, yet still the MGB need not cause a traffic jam on any road, because this venerable vehicle goes around corners and maintains maximum legal 'A' road and motorway speeds along with the bulk of today's upstarts.

Take any contemporary production car which matched the MGB's 1960s production figures, and drive it a little. Shortly you may become aware of a number of cars stacked up behind you, eager to overtake. Undertake the same journey in an MGB and, short of encountering a maniac in the latest 128 valve GXTRi street racer, you need not cause a tailback. Neither will those motorists who see you wonder what you are doing in such an OLD car, because the MGB looks as good today as it did in 1962. Unlike the majority of its contemporaries, a 1962 MGB does NOT look like an old car thirty-something years on.

Your fellow driver's perception of you and your MGB differs considerably from your perception of them. Their 1990s front wheel drive cars perform so uniformly, boringly competently that you wonder just how they stay awake on any journey lasting more than a few miles. The climax of their journey is arrival at the destination. The high point of your journey is the journey – and that lasts longer.

You will doubtless encounter some today who will earnestly inform you that the MGB is not a true sports car because it is too slow and cumbersome, and that a modern sports car or even many saloon cars can perform better on the road. As a technology-dependent product, of course the MGB is out-classed by modern sports cars, just as 1960s aeroplanes and motorcycles are outclassed by their modern equivalents. The charge that the MGB is too slow is easily dismissed because the cars will rarely been seen at the head of a queue of traffic even today; the charge that the car does not handle deserves more thought.

Although the physical elements of the MGB's suspension were influenced (detrimentally) by financial constraints, the resultant set-up achieves the desired standard of handling and roadholding as befits a car of the Grand Touring class. The MGB's handling and road-holding were safe in 1962 and they are safe today. Push the car a little around the bend and it scrubs the extra speed off in safe understeer, push it too hard around a bend and it is predictable and controllable as it shifts from understeer into oversteer. There's many a sportscar which goes around corners as though on rails up to a certain speed, but which proves nigh-on uncontrollable the moment that speed is exceeded.

The proof of this is the high survival rate of the MGB. Few cars of any type survive in any great quantity longer than about ten years, but a car which handled badly or especially which held the road poorly could anticipate a far shorter life. There are probably – certainly – more 1960s MGBs on the roads of the UK today than there are any other 1960s sports car. The handling and roadholding are quite OK.

Tough and forgiving as the MGB may be, you cannot expect it to be able to tolerate neglect as might a modern car with 12,000 mile or annual service intervals. Skimp on maintenance and in the short term the car will become less reliable and perform less well – in the longer term such neglect will shorten the life of the car.

The modern car is in theory more reliable than the average MGB, but that reliability is achieved at the expense of ever-greater sophistication. When new, the modern car should be 100% reliable but, when that car becomes old, the extra componentry which in its youth made it infallible becomes a liability – just something else to go wrong. Dependence on ever-more sophisticated electronic technology makes modern cars less user-repairable. The MGB – like other motoring greats including the Morris Minor and Volkswagen Beetle – is almost infinitely user-repairable, and the MGB will still be with us when the 1994 world production of cars is reduced to a few museum pieces.

But in order to get the best from your MGB, you've got to look after it. The MGB will reward the neglectful owner with increased fuel and repair bills, increasing unreliability and – in the worse cases – an MOT failure on the grounds of expensive-to-rectify bodywork weakness. That's where this book comes in. It is designed to unravel the mysteries of maintenance but, in recognition of the fact that many MGB owners prefer to have such work carried out professionally, it tells the reader how to protect him or herself from the shabby practices still sadly evident in a few sections of the automotive repair trade.

The book – perhaps uniquely – contains what an automotive technician friend of the author described as an 'over-comprehensive' guide to dealing with non-starting engines and on-road breakdowns. In contrast to the usual over-simplified lists of instructions (flow charts) which the reader is expected to follow like an automaton when tracing faults, the author takes the alternative route of describing how the ignition and fuel systems function because – armed with this understanding – the reader is then in a position to work out what has caused a fault for him or herself. The shortcoming of flow-chart fault finders is that, although most cover the most common faults, they cannot be truly comprehensive, there

being too many potential faults and permutations of faults to be covered adequately

With a little Tender Loving Care, your MGB will start first time, every time, and it won't let you down on the road. Look after your MGB and it will look after you.

SURVIVING PURCHASE OF AN MGB

Surviving MGB ownership is one thing – surviving the purchase of the car in the first place is quite another. Along with moving house, losing your job and a death in the family, second-hand car purchase is one of the most stressful events in our lives. *MGB – Restoration/Preparation/Maintenance*, written by the same author and published by Osprey Automotive, covers MGB appraisal and purchase in great detail; and other books and pamphlets on the subject

Broken outer sill. This outer sill broke open when the hapless owner attempted to jack the car up using the jacking point! Before this happened, he was adamant that the sills on his car were sound (mistakenly believing them to have been replaced some years before – they had in fact been patched), and he could have sold the car in this terrible condition in all innocence. You really do need to be on your guard when assessing sills!

are widely available and buyers' guides appear periodically in classic car magazines. This short section describes not how to assess and buy an MGB, but gives a few pointers on how to survive the experience.

Few people ever part with a good MGB – ask yourself, would you sell a car which was fun to drive, smart, rock-solid and reliable? No, I didn't think you would. Lots of people, however, sell rotting or unreliable MGBs when the true costs of repair or restoration become apparent. These are the facts which must be faced by anyone who is contemplating buying an MGB – there is always a wide choice on the market, but an alarming proportion of the cars offered for sale are on the market simply because they need money spending on them.

Good original (un-restored and un-bodged) MGBs are becoming increasingly rare, and the chances of discovering one are so low that you could waste years looking. The author knows

The inner step of the same car appeared sound until it was hit gently – and this hole is the result. To have the sill structure including the inner step replaced professionally will probably cost you around 40-60 hours of workshop time – more if further welded repairs are found necessary (they usually are). Multiply that by the average hourly rate, add on the price of the repair panels (and a respray) and add the total to the asking price.

the whereabouts of just one original, un-welded, low-mileage '67 GT but, like most examples, this one is not for sale and probably never will be, being something of a family heirloom to be passed down from generation to generation. If you wish to buy a really smart, sound and mechanically sorted MGB other than one of the most recent black bumper examples, you will almost certainly have to look at restored examples.

Good restored MGBs and GTs are going to be expensive. This is being written in the winter of 1994, and within the last month three reports of people spending in excess of £20,000 on the professional restoration of MGB GTs have reached the author (one bill came to £25,000 – nigh-on the price tag of a new MGR V8). Such cars will be 'as new', because virtually every component from the bodyshell downwards with the exception of major mechanical components (which will be the subjects of quality reconditioning) will be renewed. To reduce the restoration costs, owners would have to retain more of the original components, though even a 'cheap' but thorough professional restoration is going to cost £15,000 upwards at 1994 prices and, having spent so much on the car, few owners would be prepared to sell cheaply.

Not all MGB restorations are as good as the external shine of the paintwork indicates: it is possible to weld steel patches onto rotten structural bodywork (which will be covered with underseal) and save a small fortune in repair panels, to 'repair' rotten external non-structural panels using glassfibre topped with bodyfiller. Tired old mechanical components can be cleaned and painted so that they look like new. All in all, it can be difficult to tell the £20,000 restoration from the sub-£5,000 tart-up. Five years on, however, the differences will be painfully apparent: patch repairs don't last for more than a few years and tend to accelerate rusting of surrounding steel, old mechanical components can fail one by one so that the car spends more of its time off the road than on.

Reluctant as we tend to be to look the proverbial gift horse in the mouth, there is a strong case for assuming that an apparently good restored MGB which is offered at a low price is in fact a bodged MGB – the gloss will wear off after a few short years, and then the new owner will be faced with repair and restoration bills.

A car does not, however, have to be locked in an air-conditioned garage for the majority of its life and only used on sunny days, nor be the subject of an expensive professional restoration in order to be good. Many MGBs are in effect restored over a period of many years, being taken off the road now and then in order that some element of bodywork or mechanical repair can be attended to. The problem with such cars is that parts of the bodywork and various mechanical and electrical components are in different stages of deterioration – you

Cartridge filter. Small details count for a lot. A clean oil filter shows that maintenance has been attended to – at least recently. The tired old plug leads do not, however, inspire much confidence. You might perceive such things only as part of a general impression of the car – your 'gut' reaction. Be guided by your gut reaction, and the same goes for your impressions of the vendor – if you're not happy, walk away.

never know what's going to fail next or when! Despite that, these are the MGBs which make good buys and which can be acquired at reasonable prices.

All genuinely good MGBs command high prices; you cannot buy a smart, sound and reliable MGB cheaply. You can, however, find a wide choice of unsound and unreliable MGBs on the market, usually dressed-up as sound and reliable cars. Rot in structural pressings is often disguised – sometimes so well that the camouflage can fool experts – mechanical, hydraulic and electrical deficiencies are similarly disguised – sawdust in the axle, thermostat removed to hide engine overheating, fuses up-rated to hide electrical faults – the list is endless.

Firstly, never ever set yourself a deadline or rush into a purchase – be the world's most reluctant buyer, a pain in the backside for vendors. You will doubtless have seen cars 're-advertised due to time wasters' – be one of those time wasters. When you go to view a car get it into your head that you're not going to buy it, you're just going for a look. Convince yourself that the car will almost certainly fall below your standards. This prepares you mentally to find faults rather than view the car through rose-tinted spectacles: it makes it easier to reject the car and it spares you that feeling of disappointment on the return journey and those nagging doubts which can affect the strongest willed among us.

The more cars you are able to view before actually making a purchase, the better, because your knowledge will grow with each car you examine and reject. When you finally find the right car, paradoxically, you may recognise that this is the car for you even before you have examined it. It will simply look and feel 'right'.

Be guided by your 'gut' reactions; if you feel in any way uncomfortable with a car or its owner, leave it. If you're simply not sure that the car you are viewing is right for you, but cannot think of any particular reason, make your excuses and walk away.

Engine plate. Reproduction vehicle identification plates (engine, body, chassis) are widely available, a fact which makes the life of the professional car thief easier by allowing MGBs to be given 'false identities' and sold as ringers. There are two safeguards. Telephone HPI Auto-data on 01722 422422. For a fee, the company will check the car against various listings of stolen cars, any which are the subject of outstanding credit. If you have problems contacting the company, your local Police Crime Prevention Officer should be able to help. The second safeguard takes time. The British Motor Industry Heritage Trust will, for a fee (telephone them on 01926 641188 to find the current cost) trace the production records for an MGB.

A scruffy engine bay. Giving a car an external respray involves quite a lot of hard work, but nothing in comparison with spraying the engine bay – there are simply so many components to be stripped out that few people would attempt the job on a DIY basis, and others are put off by the high costs of having the job undertaken by professionals. If the car you are viewing has a freshly painted or a smart engine bay, rest assured that the vendor (or a professional restorer) has put a lot of work into the car and they are unlikely to let it go cheaply.

DEALING WITH THE VENDOR

If a vendor turns out to be 'pushy'; if he or she talks incessantly about the car's good points then the reason is probably to distract your attention from some fundamental fault, which could range from camouflaged body rot or collision damage through to something simple to rectify and trivial, but which is invariably going to cost the new owner money. If the vendor attempts to pressurise you into making a decision by saying that someone else is interested in the car this is usually an attempt to get you to buy without properly checking the car over. In both cases, walk away.

Always take along an experienced mechanic or restorer or – at the very least, a long-term

Test emissions. If you or a friend possess one of these handy little emissions testers, they can tell you a lot about the standard of maintenance a car has received, and can help highlight possible looming problems such as bore wear due to too rich a mixture or possible bearing damage due to too lean a mixture causing long-term pre-ignition.

MGB owner – when you go to view a car, because there is simply too much to take in during one viewing, and your companion can usually be relied upon to spot anything you miss. If you don't know much about mechanical matters, book the car in for an MOT – no vendor could rightly object to this. Even better, pay a professional restorer or mechanical engineer to assess the car for you – this can save you plenty in the long run.

Unless you seek a rare variant of the MGB, look locally for cars; many of the cars advertised as being in good condition actually turn out to be rotten or neglected, which is not too much of a disappointment unless you've travelled a hundred miles to see them!

WHEN YOU GET THE CAR HOME

Don't set out on a long 'test' drive – that's asking for trouble. Get the car into your garage and give it a full service, then have a number of short 'shakedown' runs of no more than a few miles' duration, so that if there are any looming problems, they will occur close enough to your home to be dealt with quickly and cheaply. You're committed now, take it easy!

CHAPTER ONE

MGB – The Great Survivor

The MGB is the last of an illustrious line of Abingdon-built MG cars with a fine sporting heritage and highly regarded the world over. Yet MG as a company was never truly an entity, never master of its own destiny, but from the outset was in effect treated like a less than favourite child which was never allowed to grow up and make its own decisions in life – governed by external, sometimes self-serving and often downright unfriendly influences.

In the early 1920s, the Morris car company possessed a separate division which was known as Morris Garages, through which the company sold its range of saloon and touring cars in the Oxfordshire area. The head of Morris Garages was Cecil Kimber, and under his leadership this division started to sell special Morris Cowleys which its craftsmen had fitted with more sporting bodywork. Morris Garages began to achieve considerable success with the marketing of these improved versions of the more staid Cowley, and the cars initially carried both Morris and MG badges, the initials MG standing for 'Morris Garages'. The MG name, one of the best known and respected names in motoring and motor sport, was born. The MG Car Company was founded in 1928 and, needless to say, the Morris badge was soon discarded to leave the MG badge in pride of place.

From the outset, MG cars were something special, something out of the ordinary. In 1928 the up-market six cylinder MG 18/80 and, perhaps more significantly, the first MG Midget, were launched. The Midget was a departure from previous MG cars in that it was a cheap and cheerful motor, whereas the earlier cars had been relatively expensive. The first Midget was a great success and set the scene for MG's future as a motor manufacturer because, since that time, although the company has produced saloon cars, MG has been best known as a manufacturer of affordable sporting cars.

In 1932 the J2 was launched, to be followed by the 'T' series which, apart from the war years, continued in production until the 1950s. Although during this lengthy period the range evolved in terms of performance, the basic layout of the cars remained close to the original design features first introduced in the J2 and which characterised the pre-war sports car. Some elements of this design can still be perceived in today's ever-popular Morgan production sports cars, and the basic lines established by the J2 still grace a number of modern kit cars.

Despite the fact that the MG Car Company did not itself go racing until the 1950s, from an early period in the company's history one-off specials were constructed to order for use in various competitions by private individuals, and these enjoyed many successes. Thus began the close association between MG and racing.

After the war, the company resumed production of the 'T' series with the TC, some of which were sold to export markets including North America. The following TD sold in quantity in the huge American market, and the significance of this sales success was not to be lost on MG's new masters. In 1952, MG, along with the bulk of the British motor industry, had been incorporated into the British Motor Corporation. Despite the fact that it was MG sports cars which had enjoyed the first American export successes, the BMC inexplicably looked elsewhere for a 'corporate' sports car to spearhead their export efforts. Prototypes were commissioned from a number of independent companies, and the Austin Healey 100 was selected.

The MG Car Company was possibly unaware that these corporate manoeuvres were taking

MGA. The MGA is an undeniably beautiful sports car. There is no more to be said, other than the fact that the Author would dearly love to own one.

place, and had itself designed a more modern sports car and then built a prototype, designated EX (EXperimental) 175. Nowadays we would all instantly recognise EX175 as the MGA, a car which was to achieve significant success with sales exceeding 100,000; but one which was to be shelved for three years by order of the corporation whilst the Healey 100 was produced. To add insult to injury, the MG company had from 1957 to manufacture the very car which had stood in the way of its own MGA. It would be mischievous of the author to point out that total sales of the 'Big' Healey (100/4 launched in 1953 through to 3000 Mk.3 discontinued in 1968) were just 70,000 in fifteen years of production, whereas the MGA sold over 100,000 in a mere five years of production.

In addition to manufacturing special cars for privateers to go racing and compete in trials, from the early 1930s MG had produced cars for privateer attempts on various speed records. The successes enjoyed by these specials had greatly boosted MG's reputation as a sports car manufacturer (which makes the BMC decision to launch a new sports car marque in Austin Healey even more difficult to understand), and this reputation was to be continued and built upon throughout the 1950s as

the company began to produce a range of streamlined EX cars to challenge (and to set new) land speed records.

The first MG prototype to resemble the MGA had been the EX 172, a special built onto a TD chassis for the 1949 Le Mans. The use of the TD chassis had given a rather high seating position, and when EX 175 (the prototype MGA) was designed, a new chassis was incorporated to overcome this problem. In 1955 MG were permitted finally to place the MGA in production.

MGA production was limited by the chassis-based construction of the car; quite simply, the company could not build the cars fast enough! The obvious solution was to design a new car which did not possess a separate chassis but which was instead of monocoque construction. In this, the body is a unit which contains integral chassis-like members onto which the suspension, engine and drive are all bolted. Such a bodyshell could be completed by a specialist manufacturer, leaving the MG factory merely to assemble components into the car, whereas in the case of the MGA, the factory had to perform some welding on the chassis before it could be used, causing the production bottleneck. The monocoque bodyshell also has the advantage of being lighter than the combined body/chassis weight of a chassis-based car.

Happily, a huge pressed steel plant opened close to MG's Abingdon home, and the company began serious development work to find a worthy successor to the MGA. It appears that the then General Manager of MG and obviously a man of some taste, John Thornley, was inspired by the shape of the Aston Martin DB2/4, and decided that this should be the starting point for the new MG. Other sentiments ascribed to John Thornley included the notion that the MGB would be in effect a poor man's Aston Martin and that the later MGB GT should be a car which no Managing Director would be ashamed to leave in his car park. In fact, it appears possible that the MGB was initially conceived as a fastback tourer, which might go some way towards explaining why the later GT version looked so good.

The MGB was to be a more luxurious car than its predecessor, with the smoother and softer ride which befits a Grand Tourer rather than the typically harsh ride of an out and out sportscar. The MGA had side screens, the MGB was to have wind-up windows. The MGA interior was spartan, the MGB was to be well appointed and even have a lockable glove compartment. The design of the MGB was also reportedly influenced by EX181 – MG's last record-breaking car which had been driven by Stirling Moss to no less than 5 Class 'F' speed records in 1957 and by Phil Hill (after its engine had been enlarged from 1498cc to 1506cc) to 6 Class 'E' records the following year.

The shape of the MGB was also heavily influenced by financial constraints and the high costs of initial tooling-up. Start-up costs would have to be kept to a level which would allow the project to break even in the shortest possible time, in order that a few years' sales could generate an acceptable profit before the MGB was replaced. Happily, the MGB shape was 'right', as time would tell.

The mechanical aspects of the MGB's design were heavily influenced by finance. Originally, the car was designed for and tested with a coil spring and radius arm rear suspension (though not independent rear suspension) to improve the ride over that of the leaf-sprung, live axle MGA. In the case of leaf spring suspension, in order to obtain a reasonable amount of axle travel and hence a comfortable ride, the springs have to be quite long. This unfortunately allows too much axle response to sudden applications of power to the rear wheels, causing tramp, in addition to poor lateral location under extreme cornering.

The coil spring arrangement initially tested on the MGB had problems. Some means was required of preventing the axle assembly from moving from side to side; and two common solutions are the Watts linkage and the Panhard Rod. When tested with a Watts linkage the suspension performed satisfactorily, but this solution was ruled out on the grounds of cost. When a less expensive Panhard Rod was tested, it caused rear wheel steer. The car appeared with leaf springs and live axle.

A number of engine options were considered but ruled out before the enlarged 1800cc B series unit was chosen. Amongst the alternatives, a new 2 litre V4 then under development (also to be available as a V6), was perhaps the most notable. It was ruled out on cost grounds. One wonders whether the flitch panels of the Mk.1 MGB which, with a little modification, can accommodate the Rover V8 engine, were originally designed with the V4 or V6 in mind.

The MGB was launched at the 1962 Motor Show; the latest and the last all-new car from a long line of Abingdon-built sporting two seater MGs. The 1962 MGB offered a 103 mph top speed and a 0-60 mph time of just over 12 seconds – not startling performance but very creditable at the time when the average saloon car 0-60 mph time was probably twice that of the MGBs and when many cars were pushed to see a top speed of 80 mph – and also quite good

The early GT, like the first of any line of cars, is the purest of the breed, though in many respects later versions best it, and many people prefer the improvements in comfort, style and mechanical sophistication of later cars.

performance per pound sterling. The car cost £949; cheaper sports cars generally offered less performance and more expensive cars generally offered progressively better speed. In other words, the price was right!

Although the MGB was far more luxurious than the MGA, the heater was an optional extra, as were the oil cooler, the front anti-roll bar and a special cushion for using the space behind the front seats for seating children. An overdrive was later offered as an optional extra.

The MGB was fitted with a three bearing crankshaft version of the B series engine (18 GA), which had a larger bore to give 1800cc. Although the three bearing engine revved freely, the unit was destined to be fitted to the Austin 1800 saloon and, in order to improve smoothness, a five main bearing version (18 GB) was developed which would later be fitted to the MGB. The gearbox had synchromesh on second, third and fourth gears.

The MGB was well received by the motoring public, and its first full year's production was a record for any MG car. Those criticisms which did surface were generally concerned with the softer suspension which made the car more of

a tourer than an out-and-out sportscar, but because the handling characteristics had purposely been 'designed into' the car rather than being an accident of production, the criticism could not have hurt too much at Abingdon.

That the MGB should one day be available in a closed version was perhaps inevitable, given the original inspiration of the Aston Martin DB2/4. Styling exercises based on the MGA back in the late 1950s had produced scale models of a car which bore some resemblance to the MGB GT, but which had a lower roof line and which looked good but not quite 'right'. MG simply could not get the GT to look the way they wanted it and so they sought the help of Pininfarina (who had previously worked on the Austin A40 – the similarity shows when you stop and think about it), who quite simply raised the windscreen and roof height to produce one of the best looking cars of the 1960s. Put simply, the MGB GT is one of those rare cars which have such perfect balance of design that they look superb from every angle.

Like the MGB, the MGB GT was given the warmest of receptions by enthusiasts and press alike, not just for its looks but also because

MGC. Larger wheels and the bonnet bulge give the MGC an arguably more aggressive appearance than the 'friendly' MGB, but the performance of the C is not so much the 'rip up the tarmac' variety as 'keep going all day at high speed with leisurely engine revs' type.

MGC engine bay. The six cylinder engine is a tight fit in the bay. Even after throwing away the MGB cross member and fitting a scalloped welded-in version in place, the bonnet still had to bulge in order to accommodate this deep unit.

many believed the handling to be slightly better than that of the original roadster. It may be true that the handling was slightly improved by the weight distribution and the extra rear springing of the GT. There were other differences.

The GT was fitted with the quieter Salisbury axle from the outset, whereas this was not fitted to the roadster until 1967. The GT had a front anti-roll bar as standard whereas the roadster had not. Top speed was up slightly due to the better aerodynamics of the GT's fixed roof, although acceleration times were up slightly owing to the extra weight.

In 1967, the Mk.2 MGB and MGB GT were launched. Although on the surface there was very little to distinguish these from the Mk.1 variants (reversing lights and better seats), under the skin there were more fundamental differences. The transmission tunnel was widened (to accept the gearbox for the MGC) and underneath it there lay a four synchromesh gearbox. The electrics were changed to negative earth and the dynamo was replaced with a more efficient alternator. Nothing was done to improve the handling or roadholding, and nothing was done to upgrade the engine power. In fact, export cars destined for the

North American market were subjected to the first of an ever more restrictive series of exhaust emission control modifications. The earliest of these had but a mild effect on performance, although later legislative requirements would seriously affect the performance of the engine.

With production of the Austin Healey (which by then sported a 6 cylinder three litre engine) ending in 1967, MG launched the short-lived MGC and MGC GT. In an effort to gain performance, the MGC was fitted with a straight 6 cylinder engine which, with a capacity of 2,912cc, gave over a quarter more flywheel BHP than the 1800cc B engine. Unfortunately, it was also not only very much heavier than the B series engine, but also so much taller that the front suspension cross member had to be dispensed with, along with the rest of the front suspension. The massive standard cross member was replaced by a welded in fabrication, and the suspension was replaced by adjustable torsion bar springing (similar in basic design to that of the Morris Minor) allied to telescopic dampers.

The weight of the C series engine brought another drawback. If you increase the weight at the front end of a car too much, then the result can be increased understeer – the desire of the mass of the car to carry on in a straight line despite the efforts of the tyres to steer it around the corner – and the MGB was an understeering car even with the lighter 1800cc B series engine. As a rally car, the MGC was not exactly the obvious choice, but for mile-eating touring in the grand style the MGC was, and still is, a very competent performer. The MGC was discontinued in 1969 after a production life which saw just 8,999 cars produced. Today it is deservedly a cult car.

The next attempt to give the now elderly (in sports car terms) MGB extra 'zip' came after the company had noted the successes of one Frank Costello in fitting the mighty 3,500cc ex-Buick Rover V8 engine into the car. This unit offered far more power than even the C series engine and had the priceless advantage of weighing – with all ancillaries – very little more than the original B series engine. Frank Costello fitted the 150BHP Rover car version, whereas the factory alternative utilised the 135BHP version as used in the Range Rover.

It has been suggested by some that Mr Costello experienced certain difficulties in obtaining V8 engines after the factory V8 had arrived – the implication being that the group were shutting out this unwelcome competition; in fact Mr Costello was not alone, because MG reportedly could never acquire them in quantity, and just 2,591 examples were produced. Today, V8 MGBs are more numerous than ever because a growing number of companies and individuals have discovered that it is not too difficult a task to fit a V8 engine – usually salvaged from a Rover SD1 – into the average MGB.

In 1975, the character of the MGB (along with that of the MGB's smaller stable-mate, the Midget) was brutally changed by the need to meet new North American crash regulations. These dictated that the lighting system should not be impaired following a 5mph crash, and furthermore, that bumpers should be at a regulation height. It says much for the popularity of the MGB and the difficulty of creating an all-new car to meet these requirements that the Group decided to persevere with the MGB. The upshot of the work needed to comply with the new regulations was that nearly a hundredweight of extra metal (covered in black urethane, giving rise to the name 'rubber/black bumper' MGB) was attached where the chrome bumpers used to be, and that the ride height was increased. These alterations were about the last thing the MGB needed. The car already rolled to a degree when cornering, and raising the centre of gravity *and* the weight of the car accentuated matters. The extra weight needed to meet the crash regulations took the heavier GT into a higher emission class with more stringent emission requirements than the roadster's class, and so the GT was dropped from the North American market.

The ever-faithful MG enthusiasts were initially horrified that so elegant a car could have such appendages arbitrarily thrust upon it to meet the requirements of a legislation-bound overseas market. Yet with the passage of time, even such deep wounds heal, and today the rubber bumper MGB and MGB GT are widely regarded as classic in every sense of the word.

MG started work on a replacement for the MGB; ADO 21 – a mid-engined beauty (actually, it was the Austin Maxi engine) with

In its dotage, the MGB was not capable of showing a clean pair of heels to many cars, having put on weight, got out of shape and having had the life progressively throttled out of it to meet US regulations. Worse, some cars – including small cars and family saloons – were developed over the years to the point at which they could out-drag, out top speed and yet be more economical on fuel than the MGB. No matter, it's a 'real' MGB and its owners love it.

The early MGBs have masses of unused internal volume under the bonnet. One engine option was to fit a V4 under development in Australia, which probably explains why the MGB engine bay can accommodate the Rover V8.

Later versions lost the mechanically driven fan, but extra sophistication under the bonnet made it a far more crowded environment.

Later cars became ever-more plush, further and further away from what constitutes a sports car and closer to the Grand Touring class.

The early dashboard was simple and uncluttered.

As the chrome bumper car aged, its dash became more crowded but nonetheless looks 'right' for a British sports car.

MGR V8. One second after midnight on Tuesday, 13th October 1992, Rover Cars lifted the embargo on this and other photographs of the MGR V8 – and the motoring world went wild. Americans - denied the opportunity to buy the original MGB V8 – are denied the chance to acquire the MGR V8 (and, reportedly, the planned mid-engined MG of 1995).

OK, it's an MGB which has put on muscle and dressed itself in a sharp new suit – the press almost to a man deride it for not being a TVR, but MGR V8 owners the author has spoken to love the car.

Lotus-esque lines but which would have been quite expensive to put into production. Instead, the Corporate decision was to spend far less development funding on the new Triumph TR7, of which, one automotive designer of note allegedly uttered the immortal words "My God! Have they done the same to the other side?". Enough said.

In the 1990s, motoring pundits are gazing with awe at the Mazda MX5, pronouncing it to be the 'new MGB' and lamenting those boardroom decisions which firstly strangled development of the MGB and latterly gave it the chop. Quite right, too.

Now we have the MGR V8 which is to herald the start of a new line of MG sports cars. As this is written towards the end of 1994, unofficial confirmation of the development of an all-new MG sports car is not too hard to tease out of some Rover staff, but detailed information is not available. Speculation amongst motoring journalists is rife – the car will be mid-engined, will be closer to Midget size than MGB – and, it seems, Rover have learnt the value of teasing maximum publicity from an excitable motoring press for cars which do not officially exist. The only response the author garnered from Rover Public Affairs was that the press speculation is not 100% correct, and that the new MG will hold a few surprises for the press launch. By the time this book is published, I can but hope that MG fans will have the option of buying a new MG sports car which is thoroughly modern where it counts, yet which still retains the tradition of MG as a marque.

The MGR V8 is to have a strictly limited production run of just 2,000 cars – 591 fewer than the original MGB GT V8, itself quite a rare classic. As far as Rover Cars are concerned, when the two thousandth car is driven off the production line that's it – no more. But the MGB need not be allowed to 'die' again.

The MGB spares and other connected businesses have a turnover of millions of pounds in the UK alone; if the major players were to pool their resources and work together on a common project, surely it would not be beyond them to fit out a Heritage shell with a modern engine and gearbox, independent rear suspension and improvements in damping and braking, and to set up a small scale assembling facility which follows the (at the time of writing) current motor industry trend towards niche marketing? Sadly, stifling global legislation (a lesser version of which brought about the demise of the original MGB in 1981) for all new cars will probably prevent such a re-birth from occurring.

But the original MGB will continue to survive, just as it has over the twelve years since the cessation of its production. During this period, the survival potential of the MGB has actually improved through the growing restoration industry dedicated to keeping as many examples as possible on the road.

COMPETITION

The MGB was never a wildly successful competition car. It was campaigned at Le Mans, Sebring, Brands Hatch, Nurburgring and elsewhere; it was entered in a multitude of rallies

from the Monte Carlo downwards. Usually the MGBs finished, often they won their respective classes, occasionally they emerged outright victors. Why was the car never a world-beater? The truth may be that the MGB was never really given the necessary competition development to excel at any particular type of event. Despite this handicap, the MGB was, in its own way, a hugely successful competition car. Not too many cars can have won their class in the Monte Carlo rally and also in prestigious world-class endurance track events – in both cases when pitted against the world's finest machinery. Not too many cars can boast the sheer versatility of the MGB as a competition car.

Firstly, let's consider the question of development with an eye on the Monte Carlo rally and the modern equivalent of that rally, the Pirelli – now the Mitsubishi – classic. In the Monte Carlo's of the 1960s the MGB was always a bridesmaid to the Mini Cooper S brides, which were at that time indisputably the world's finest rally vehicles. Yet in today's Pirelli Classic Marathon, when all entries are privateers and the preparation work is roughly the same for all cars, we find that the MGBs are neatly splitting or beating the 1275cc Mini Cooper S's in the results list.

If the MGB can be retrospectively recognised as a potential world-class 1960s rally car, what of track events? Well, the MGB did excel at endurance races due to its reliability, which kept the MGBs going when some of the fancy, overstressed buzz-boxes were dropping by the wayside. The greatest hurdle faced by the MGB in track events was not the fact that it was in direct competition with Ferraris, Porsches, Cobras and the like, but something called Corporate Policy which dictated that the competitions department should make do with very limited resources when competitors were throwing vast amounts of money into research and development for their race cars – almost as though racing success helped to sell production cars.

As the 1960s progressed, motor manufacturers who took competition seriously developed new engines, suspension and even new cars in order to win, because winning was (commercially) everything. The MGB was competing with cars like the Shelby Cobra, Ford GT40 and Ferrari P330, plus even more exotic machinery which was manufactured purely to win these events. While the cars of competitors were taking great strides in the evolution of the sports racing car, still the under-developed MGB valiantly competed with no loss of honour and with occasional success.

If the MGB deserves any competition accolade, then it must surely be for the most versatile competition car which happened to be forced to fight with both hands tied behind its back and still occasionally won...

As recent rallies have shown, the car is still winning. Both as a production car and a competition car, the MGB is the great survivor.

The Marathon de La Route in 1966, an 84-hour race at Nurburgring. The car crashed on the first lap, destroying three of the four spotlights. Two replacements were jury-rigged to the grille, which explains the tatty front end in Keith Woodcock's painting! Despite the early mishap, the car was first overall, driven by Andrew Hedges (who commissioned this work to commemorate the victory) and Julian Vernaeve.

CHAPTER TWO

Survival for (and in) your MGB

The MGB is an outstandingly robust and (usually) reliable classic sports car which is capable of being driven hard for huge mileages before serious remedial attention is needed to mechanical components. All MGBs are, however, now old cars and, like old people, they require more in the way of care and attention if they are to remain fit and healthy. Those owners who neglect simple regular servicing routines will suffer increased mechanical component wear which will not only shorten the life-span of many components but also increase the likelihood of on-road breakdowns occurring.

A properly cared-for car which is driven hard will usually outlive and be far more reliable than a neglected car which is driven gently and infrequently. Caring for your MGB entails more than regular servicing, though, and a little time spent regularly maintaining the external bodywork, the brightwork and the underside of the car will pay handsome dividends in the long run, because such maintenance fends off the day when body restoration will be needed.

Caring for the interior is also worthwhile, especially for those whose cars possess the original interior trim, because such cars are invariably worth more and will become increasingly rarer and more sought-after than cars fitted with modern reproduction interiors. If your car has leather seats then periodically cleaning, feeding and sealing them using proprietary kits will keep them looking good. Vacuum cleaning dirt out of the carpets regularly will increase their life span.

Mechanical servicing breaks down into three areas: the first concerns a number of regular checks which can reveal problems before they arise, the second encompasses those tasks

which can be tackled easily and quickly by people who possess a minimum of special tools and no mechanical nor technical knowledge, and the third concerns those jobs which require a modicum of experience and special equipment. The first and second areas should be within the ability of any able-bodied person and include a range of checks and maintenance of lubricant and fluid levels; the third area concerns those tasks touching upon the ignition and carburation.

The checks which are made during basic servicing might reveal the need for more complicated repair work, which can be carried out professionally or which the reader may care to undertake. In the latter case, it is strongly recommended that a good maintenance/repair manual is obtained.

Readers are strongly recommended to read chapter four – especially the section headed 'An Introduction to Fuel and Electrics' – before carrying out any work on their cars, whether they follow the instructions given here or in any other book or manual.

BASIC SERVICING

It is perfectly acceptable – in fact, it is a good idea for the novice DIY mechanic – to carry out basic maintenance at home, but to leave more advanced work to your local garage or service centre. The benefit of this is that basic servicing is needed on a far more regular basis than is more advanced servicing, so that instead of incurring a professional's bill every 3,000 miles or 3 months, it can be deferred to every 6,000 miles/six monthly or 12,000 miles/annually, depending on how much work you are prepared to undertake. The basic servicing routines described here do include

Jacks. The scissors jack is OK for roadside wheel changes, but for workshop use the least you should aim for is a bottle jack with a lifting capacity of two tons. Use only on firm, stable, surfaces.

Basic skills – filing. To repair rather than replace some components, tools such as a vice, files and saws are often necessary. Filing a flat surface is an art – practice on scrap steel and when you can file a simple flat, move on to trying more adventurous contours.

Basic skills – sawing. Hacksaw blades should be fitted so that they cut on the forwards stroke. Use two hands to operate a hacksaw, as shown. If you want to break a hacksaw blade, though, try using both hands at the rear of the saw – it never fails!

various checks which can reveal situations when complicated repair work requiring the use of special tools will have to be undertaken, either professionally or at home.

Basic servicing entails checking and maintaining the correct levels of fluids and lubricants, plus carrying out brake, tyre, lighting and other safety related checks. Humdrum, boring, absolutely essential tasks.

A minimum of equipment is needed, and most of this is so fundamental that every motorist should have access to it irrespective of whether he or she undertakes any maintenance work on the car. The equipment which will be required comprises a good jack (a large and stable bottle jack is acceptable but a small trolley jack is preferable), a pair of axle stands to support the car, a tyre pressure gauge and a tyre pump, a tyre tread depth gauge, a grease gun, screwdrivers, pliers and a set of imperial spanners from $1/4"$ to $3/4"$.

Those whose MGBs have wire wheels will also need a copper/rawhide mallet to undo the wheel spinners, although because such a mallet should be carried in the car at all times in case of punctures, this can hardly be considered to be special equipment. If funds permit, an imperial socket set with $1/2"$ drive will repay its cost many times over.

You will also need to keep a small stock of servicing consumables, including motor oil, axle oil, hydraulic fluid (preferably silicone), grease and anti-freeze. The costs of this equipment and consumables should be roughly equivalent to having one or two minor services carried out professionally, so that they are soon recouped. If the above lists appear a little daunting to those who have never carried out any work on their cars, bear in mind that every motorist should ideally possess everything contained in the list, irrespective of whether they intend to work on their cars or whether the need to work on the car is forced upon them by circumstance: say, the car refusing to start one morning or the need temporarily to fix

some fault so that the car can be driven in safety to the service centre.

The first servicing example which springs to most people's minds is changing the engine oil. This is an extremely simple (if sometimes messy) operation, but an essential one. As engine oil ages, it loses its ability to properly lubricate metal surfaces which move in contact with other metal surfaces. There are many such metal to metal bearing areas in a car engine, and when the oil loses its ability to properly lubricate them, they wear very quickly indeed because they come into contact with each other, whereas they should be separated by a very thin film of oil. Rapid wear of engine components means that an expensive engine rebuild will shortly be needed. Elements of the steering gear, drive and braking mechanisms also require regular lubrication and failure to properly attend to this leads to the same consequences as failure to attend to engine oil – breakdown of the unit in question followed by expensive repair.

SAFETY

When raising and supporting the car, only do so on a flat, firm and crumble-proof surface such as concrete or asphalt (in hot weather, protect the asphalt using thick plywood boards or something similar to prevent the jack and axle stands from digging into the surface). Always place chocks both front and aft of the two wheels which are to remain on the ground before raising the car. If the car has a steering lock then engage it before raising the rear end of the car by turning the steering wheel until it locks – then chock the wheels. Never work on the car when it is supported only by the jack (roadside wheel changes excepted), but lower it onto sturdy axle stands. A jack is a lifting device and is not intended to support heavy weights like the MGB; furthermore, the car is not sufficiently stable when supported only by a jack, it needs two solid supports.

When you raise the front of the car, you can place the axle stands either under the main cross member (with wood padding) or under the chassis rails. When you raise the rear of the car, place axle stands under the axle or – only if you intend to remove the leaf springs and/or axle – under the front of the spring hanger brackets.

Raising the car. The author raises the rear of the car using his small trolley jack located under the differential casing. Note that he keeps the jack at arm's length – just in case the car decides to topple off the jack. Both front wheels are in the 'dead ahead' position and chocked fore and aft. Always lower the car slowly.

Car supported on axle stands – crossmember. Having raised the front end of the car (jack located under the towing eye bracket on the crossmember), the author has placed axle stands under the sturdy wishbone pivots.

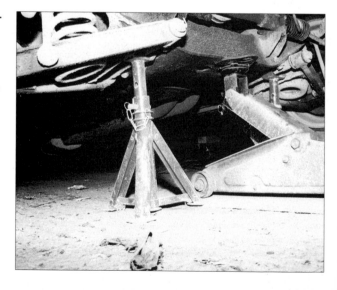

Car supported on axle stands – chassis rails. An alternative axle stand location is under the main chassis members, which leaves plenty of working space under the front end.

Car supported on axle stands – spring hanger. The leaf spring front hanger bracket can be used (preferably with wood packing).

Car supported on axle stands rear – under axle. The axle is the obvious place for axle stands – unless, that is, you're going to remove the axle or springs, in which case (top right)...

Wheel chocked. Ideally, chocks are wedge-shaped but, if you have to chock a wheel for a roadside wheel change, use anything which comes to hand. Bricks, balks of timber – anything is better than nothing.

WEEKLY CHECKS

ENGINE OIL The engine oil level is checked using the dipstick, situated on the offside of the engine block. The engine should not have been running for some time so that the oil is drained properly into the sump. Take a clean rag in one hand, then pull the dipstick upwards with the other hand, and wipe the oil from the lower end of the dipstick. Replace the dipstick, then withdraw it again and hold it horizontally. There are two marks on the dipstick, indicating the maximum and minimum acceptable oil level. If the level is too low, top it up through the rocker box cover filler, but do not pour in too much at this stage, because if you do then the excess will have to be removed (which is messy). Leave the oil for a minute or two to drain down into the sump, then wipe the dipstick clean and again test the oil level, topping up again if necessary. In practice, once you have established a set service routine, the oil level should not need topping up. If the oil level is found to be regularly low then it is being burned or lost in some way, and you should either consult a good repair manual or (preferably) seek professional advice.

Should you inadvertently over-fill the sump, it will be necessary to drain off the excess. This is achieved by placing a suitable receptacle under the sump plug (an old 5 litre oil tin with a side cut out is ideal), removing the plug for a few seconds to allow a little of the oil to drain and then re-fitting the plug. If you drain too much oil in this way, then top up the engine using fresh oil – never re-use old engine oil.

COOLANT The engine should be cold. Remove the radiator cap and visually check the level of the coolant, topping up if necessary. If the coolant level has dropped significantly, then some has been lost and the reason should be discovered as soon as possible. External leakage is usually visible as staining from the anti-freeze, or by bringing the engine to working temperature and looking to see where coolant escapes. Check all hoses and their connections; if a hose is found to be leaking then replace it immediately, because it could burst in the near future, drain the system of coolant and

Dashpot oil. Fill the dashpot to within $^1/2"$ of the top. Ideally, you will use a special lubricant for this, though most people make do with ordinary motor oil.

Start off by cleaning the engine bay if it is dirty – maintenance and repair work is so much more pleasant as a result of a few minutes extra work.

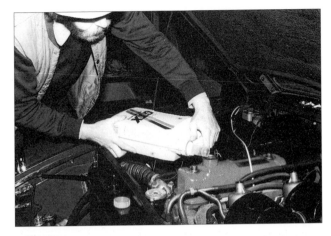

Topping up engine oil. When using a five litre oil container, offer it up horizontally as shown, so that you have control over the flow of oil. Don't pour in too much – pour a little, test the sump level using the dipstick, then pour in a little more until the level is correct.

Radiator cap removal. Even after taking the precaution of feeling the top hose for pressure, press down on the radiator cap as you twist it – you will feel whether there is any pressure left in the system. Remove the cap slowly and angle it away from you – just in case. The author may seem a little over-cautious about radiator cap removal; this is because he once (many years ago) collected a face full of scalding coolant!

Feeling top hose. This is the top hose. When the coolant becomes hot, the system is pressurised – not very much, but sufficient to blow scalding water all over anyone foolish enough to remove the radiator cap before the pressure has dropped! The coolant can become highly pressurised if the head gasket leaks, but that's another story. Squeeze the top hose to feel whether the system still has pressure – when the pressure disappears, remove the radiator cap.

leave you and the car stranded. Staining on the radiator fins obviously indicates a faulty core – various proprietary liquids are available to seal such small holes, but the problem really requires professional attention; either the radiator should be re-cored or exchanged for a reconditioned unit. Engine internal coolant losses are serious and professional advice should be sought immediately.

In sufficiently low temperatures, water, which makes up the bulk of coolant, freezes solid, and if the coolant in your engine is permitted to freeze then the resultant expansion can be sufficient to crack the main (cylinder) block. If this happens, the easiest solution is to have an exchange engine fitted at considerable cost.

To prevent coolant from freezing, an anti-freeze solution is added in a strength to match the kind of temperatures which are likely to be encountered. The solution of anti-freeze needed is as follows (temperatures given in degrees Fahrenheit); 9 degrees 25% anti-freeze, -2 degrees 33% antifreeze, -33 degrees 50% antifreeze. As winter and colder temperatures approach, it is as well to take your car to a service centre and ask for the anti-freeze mixture to be checked and topped up to a suitable strength if necessary, or to drain the system and re-fill it with water and new anti-freeze.

Radiator drain tap. Some radiators are fitted with drain taps – this one simply screws in and out. Check the condition of the copper sealing ring and replace if necessary.

WHEELS/TYRES With the car on its road wheels, check the tyre pressures (given in the appendices). If the pressure of any tyre is unduly low then it will pay to remedy the problem and bring the spare tyre into play while the faulty unit is attended to. Slow leaks never cure themselves, they deteriorate in time and having one tyre with low pressure is not only an offence in most countries but it jeopardises handling and road-holding. Check the tyres for cuts, abrasions, bulges and to ensure that they have nothing sticking into them. Also check the pressure of the spare tyre.

Check also the security of the wheel nuts or the spinners.

BRAKE/CLUTCH FLUID Unscrew the caps from the brake and clutch reservoirs, keeping a clean piece of cloth handy to mop up any spillage of fluid, because this is an excellent paint remover. It is not difficult to stuff a piece of rag under the reservoirs to catch any stray fluid if your hands aren't too steady! If, incidentally, you carry out or have carried out any repairs to the clutch or brake hydraulic system which involve draining all of the fluid, then you have the option of replacing the old fluid with more expensive modern silicone fluids, and these are highly recommended because they don't absorb water, they don't need periodic replacement, they aren't so highly flammable and they don't strip paint.

Checking tyre pressures using compressor. If you use a compressor to inflate your tyres, it is worth checking the built-in gauge to ensure it gives accurate readings. The same goes for foot pumps with built-in gauges – these can sometimes prove very inaccurate.

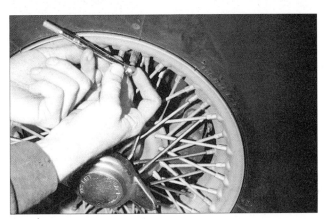

A small tyre pressure gauge costs just a few pounds and should last for years. Those with built-in dials should be more accurate than the push-out type shown here, though either should be more than accurate enough.

Checking spare. Don't forget to check the pressure in the spare tyre regularly!

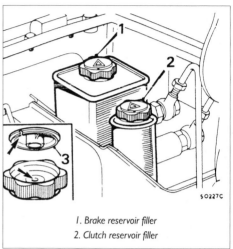

1. Brake reservoir filler
2. Clutch reservoir filler

Master cylinders. Topping up the master cylinders. In theory, this should not be necessary – the clutch and brake hydraulic systems should not lose fluid. In practice, a tiny loss of fluid is not uncommon – check that it is not leaking from wheel cylinders, calliper piston seals, hoses or unions.

The clutch and brake master cylinders as fitted to early cars. Note that the caps have built-in breathers – should these become blocked, the fluid would not be able to replace any which was lost and, over a period of time, the situation could become dangerous. (Courtesy Autodata).

Check that the levels in each reservoir have not dropped since the last check. If a level has dropped very slightly then top it up and make a note to check it again in a day or two in order to ensure that the small initial loss is not the start of a major loss. If the level of either has dropped substantially (more than about $1/4$" to $3/8$ ") then top it up but investigate the cause at the earliest opportunity, because the lost fluid could be contaminating the brakes, it could be leaking into an area where it creates a fire hazard (most hydraulic fluids are highly inflammable), and in any event it will continue – if left unattended – to culminate in the total loss of brakes or clutch.

In the interests of safety, unless you have considerable experience in repair work, it may well be best to have this problem checked out professionally.

Check the windscreen washer fluid level.

Later cars had a servo. This uses a vacuum from the inlet manifold to assist the braking effort – it does not make the brakes more effective – it merely reduces the amount of pedal effort necessary for a given level of braking effort. Problems with the servo will be apparent immediately as a sudden need for very high pedal pressures to achieve braking effort. Though servos can be repaired or serviced at home, the work is perhaps best left to professionals, or a faulty unit replaced altogether.

This late Roadster has an electric fan – but most people still refer to the generator drive belt as the 'fan' belt. When this belt is correctly tensioned, the deflection under firm thumb pressure should be ¹/4" on the longest run.

Dynamo bolts. Slacken the bracket nut first, then these two nuts and bolts.

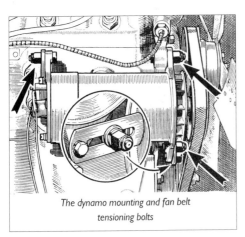

The dynamo mounting and fan belt tensioning bolts

Tensioning fan belt. There are three nuts, one threaded stud and two bolts securing the generator. (Courtesy Autodata).

Tensioning fan belt. The author uses a large screwdriver as a lever to pull the generator and hence tension the drive belt: whilst pressure is applied, the bracket nut can be pinched up, followed by the others.

MONTHLY

Carry out all of the checks already outlined, and supplement them with the following.

FAN BELT The fan belt connects the crank-shaft pulley, the generator and the water pump; it also (on early cars) drives the engine cooling fan. On later cars, the fan is electrically driven. The belt is more properly called the 'generator drive belt' – but it is still generally referred to as the 'fan belt'.

Check the deflection: if, by applying firm pressure with your thumb half-way along the longest run of the belt, the belt deflects by more than $1/2''$ (engine-driven fan) or $1/4''$ (cars with electric fans), then slacken the gen-erator nuts, apply leverage against the genera-tor in order to tension the belt and re-tighten the nuts whilst keeping the belt under tension.

GEARBOX Early MGBs. Lift any carpeting or other cover from the transmission tunnel behind the radio speaker support panel, under which you will find a black rubber bung. Remove this, and from underneath within the transmission tunnel it is just possible for those with slim fingers to reach and withdraw the gearbox oil level dipstick. A tip worth passing on is to tie a length of strong cotton to the dipstick handle, and to lead this through the access hole – the bung will be no more difficult to fit – to make removal of the dipstick easier in future.

Later MGBs. There is an oil filler/level plug situated on the side of the gearbox, so you'll have to raise one side of the car in order to check and maintain the correct oil level.

Check the level of the oil, and top up if nec-essary. With early cars, you can use a length of pipe with a small funnel at the top for this, and if just a small quantity of oil is needed to top up (and in the case of later cars), use a pumping oil can. If there has been substantial oil loss since the last check, then the cause

should be immediately investigated and reme-died. Not only the gearbox but also the over-drive (where fitted) should be checked for leakage if the oil level has dropped, although the overdrive usually gives advance notice of low gearbox oil levels because it depends on this for its operation.

AXLE The axle oil level plug is situated at the rear of the axle unit, and can be reached from under the car, although it will help if the body-work is raised slightly on a padded jack. To undo the plug requires a special tool, although a $3/8''$ square socket drive will usually do the job. The Hypoid oil should be level with the level plug hole.

BRAKES Check the handbrake travel and, if this is excessive, proceed as follows.

It is easier to adjust the brakes if the road wheels are removed; slacken the nuts or spin-ners before raising the rear of the car. Place chocks on the front wheels which are to remain on the ground and support it on axle stands. Take the opportunity to check the length of flexible brake hose for leakage at the unions, and for bulges and abrasions (if dam-aged, replace), and to check the brake back-plates for oil or brake fluid leakage.

Slacken the brake adjusters using the proper square spanner tool. If they will not turn try spraying on freeing oil, leaving this to soak into the threads then re-try. If the adjuster still refuses to turn don't resort to brute force – you'll damage the stud – the brakes will have to be stripped and the adjusters freed. Screw the adjusters back in until you feel resistance (they have pushed the shoes against the drums) then depress the foot brake pedal to centre the brake shoes. It will normally then be possible to screw the adjusters further in before resis-tance is felt. Press the brake pedal again to cen-tre the brake shoes, then check that the drum is free to rotate and, if not, slacken the adjuster concerned by one click.

If the level is down only a little, a pumping oilcan is the easiest tool for the job.

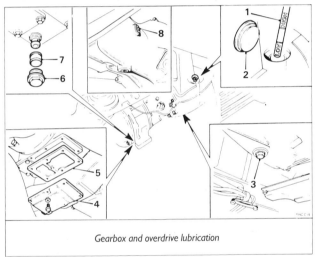

Gearbox and overdrive lubrication

Owners of later cars are not so fortunate, having to deal with a gearbox oil level plug which can only be reached from under the car. (Courtesy Autodata).

1. Gearbox dipstick (early cars)
2. Rubber plug
3. Overdrive drain plug
4. Overdrive filter cover
5. Filter
6. Relief valve plug
7. Relief valve filter
8. Gearbox filler/lever plug
   (later cars)

Axle oil level. The axle needs oil just as much as do the engine and gearbox, yet some DIY mechanics tend to neglect to keep its oil topped up. Ideally, the car will be level when the level is checked. Rather than jacking up the rear of the car, if you don't have access to a pit why not seek out an area of level ground which joins onto a downwards slope? Park the car so that the rear wheels are on the crest of the slope and you have both clearance to get at the oil level plug and a level car.

Adjusting the handbrake. You cannot adjust the handbrake too frequently – most people do it far too infrequently, only when the performance of the handbrake demands. This unfortunately leads to seized adjusters, with all the work that entails – in the worst cases, removing the adjuster and playing a flame on the body to expand it so that the adjuster can be turned. Use aluminium-based lubricant on the thread – it's wonderful stuff.

This illustrates how difficult it is to get at the handbrake adjuster with the rear wheel in situ. If you decide to remove the wheel to ease access, ensure that the car really is securely held aloft before sticking your head into the wheelarch to try and see what you are working on. If the car fell, it would probably break your neck!

You could, after greasing the exposed threads of the brake adjusters, slip a length of tight-fitting plastic hose over the exposed thread; this should prevent any future problems with stuck adjusters. (Courtesy Autodata).

Neglect to give the handbrake cable a few pumps with the grease gun periodically, and you'll probably one day have to take it off the car and spend ages working penetrating fluid into the outer in order to free it off.

Handbrake cable grease nipple. Always clean off grease nipples before using the grease gun on them – especially the handbrake cable nipple, which is invariably covered with dirt.

37

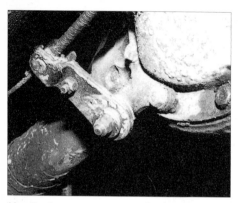

Handbrake compensator mechanism. If the compensator seizes, don't mess around – unbolt it, dismantle it, then thoroughly clean and lubricate it. A sticking handbrake will add serious money to your fuel bill!

Dynamo. Oiling the rear dynamo bearing. Don't overdo this – just a drop or two will suffice.

It is as well to test the handbrake and foot brake before using the car on the open road. This can be achieved by raising one wheel at a time and trying to turn it while the brakes are applied (not much of a test, admittedly, but it will reveal whether your brakes are really poor) or preferably by getting the car moving and testing the brakes on your driveway.

Whilst the rear of the car is raised, take the opportunity to check the tyres for damage and for tread wear. Also visually check both the brake and fuel lines for damage. Check the exhaust system for leakage, which will be apparent as small areas of carbon, visible on the outer surface – usually at one of the welded joints.

IGNITION Although it is not essential that the ignition is checked on a monthly basis, a few quick checks can highlight looming problems best dealt with at the earliest opportunity.

The condition of the sparking plugs can tell you a lot about how the engine is running, so remove these and, if you're not sure of your ability to remember which high tension lead goes to which plug, either mark them with 1,

2, 3, or 4 bands using typists' correction fluid or place temporary marking tags on them.

The plug ends should be a light fawn colour; if this is so, then check the gaps using a feeler gauge and re-fit them. If the plugs are covered with a black soot then the engine is running too rich and the carburation requires attention. If the plugs are covered with a shiny black layer (rather like tar) then oil is being burnt; the oil might be leaking past the valve stems (valve seals, possible worn guides necessitating a cylinder head overhaul) or past the piston rings, indicating piston ring damage/wear or simply long-term engine (bore) wear. In both instances, clean the plugs and set the gap before re-fitting them.

If the plugs are glazed then the engine is running too hot – the cause might be relatively trivial such as air induction or mis-set ignition timing, but the consequences are serious, so, unless you are experienced in such fault-finding, have the problem attended to professionally at the earliest opportunity. An engine which is running too hot might exhibit other symptoms such as pinking when the engine is running under load.

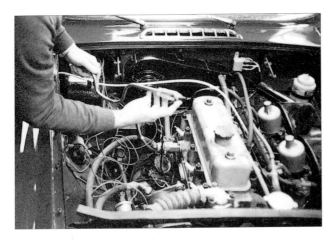

Removing spark plugs. A speed brace (supplied with most decent socket sets) should give sufficient leverage to 'start' the plugs – if not, they have either been grossly over-tightened, or they've been in there far too long.

Checking the plug gap. The gauge should drag very slightly within the gap when it has been correctly set.

Replacing plugs – starting by hand. Unless the spark plugs are too hot to handle (let them cool, which won't take long) always start them by hand. If you use a tool to start them and inadvertently cross-thread them, the head will have to come off, and a helicoil will have to be fitted – not cheap, troublesome and eminently avoidable.

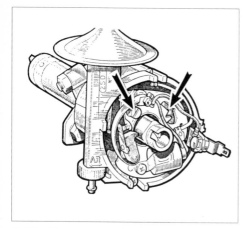

Setting the points gap. Test the points gap when the heel is resting on a lobe of the cam. To adjust the points gap, simply slacken the securing screw and use a screwdriver in the notch provided in the base plate to alter the gap. Tighten the base plate screw and re-check the gap. (Courtesy Autodata).

Oiling the distributor drive shaft. A few drops of oil should be applied to the distributor drive shaft, and also through the base plate onto the mechanical advance/retard unit. Failure to do the latter can mean a loss of performance in the long term. A seized mechanical advance should become apparent when you set the ignition timing using a stroboscope – rev the engine (vacuum advance pipe disconnected), and the mechanical system should advance the timing, which gives a little extra 'oomph' for acceleration.

Remove the distributor cap by pressing on the centre of each spring clip whilst lifting away the end. If you have not already done so, remove the sparking plugs, engage the handbrake and place the car in neutral gear. Turn the engine over using the fan blades (early cars) or – for later cars with electric fans – either using a spanner on the crankshaft pulley nut or by placing the car in fourth gear and rocking it backwards and forwards. When the ignition points are fully open, check their condition; if they are deeply pitted then they should be replaced, along with the condenser, if they are dirty then clean them. Check that the gap is correct using a feeler gauge and, if not, slacken the fixed plate screw in the base plate, adjust the gap using a screwdriver then re-tighten the screw and re-check that the gap is now correct. If the points gap is altered, then the ignition timing will have to be re-set. See 3,000 mile/ 3 monthly servicing.

KINGPINS Failure to grease the kingpins regularly will result in their rapid wear, which firstly causes stiffness and loss of self-centring effect in the steering and, long-term, dangerous play in the steering and an MOT failure.

If you don't mind grovelling around underneath the car, then you can grease the three nipples on each kingpin simply by turning the steering to full lock – first one way, then the other – and using a grease gun to pump in grease until clean grease emerges. With the steering turned to the right, you can just reach the nipples on the off-side, and vice-versa. Early cars only possessed two nipples per kingpin, but most if not all of these will by now have been fitted with a third.

The textbook method of greasing the kingpins entails raising the front of the car and removing the road wheels to improve access to the nipples – if you use this method, then support the main crossmember on axle stands and use a trolley jack to raise the spring pans to the 'on-road' position before applying the grease.

Kingpins greasing. Note; the suspension is in the 'on the road' position. This allows the grease to work its way properly into the kingpin assembly. You can either raise the car, remove the wheel and compress the suspension using a trolley jack, or simply lie in the dirt on your back (turn the wheels to full lock as necessary) in order to get the grease gun onto the three nipples.

The old grease which emerges from the assembly should be cleaned away. It's a pity to waste it, so spread it onto any nearby ferrous surface (such as the castle rail) to help prevent future rusting.

Whilst the front of the car is raised, take the opportunity to check the tyres for damage and the treads for uneven wear. If wear is concentrated on the inside or outside of the pattern, the culprit is usually the tracking – the wheels are pointing too far in or out. Have the tracking attended to professionally if necessary. If tyre wear is concentrated at the edges of the tread then the tyres are under-inflated; if wear is apparent in the middle of the tread, the tyres are over-inflated.

GENERAL Check all visible wiring for damage.

EVERY THREE MONTHS OR 3,000 MILES, SIX MONTHLY AND ANNUALLY

If you don't like getting dirty, it is advisable to consider having these services carried out professionally, because they include – among other tasks – an engine oil and filter change and suspension lubrication. It is no bad thing to check the timing and – at least annually and preferably six monthly – the carburation. If you elect to have this and other servicing carried out professionally, then there will be certain signs that show whether the jobs were all carried out properly. Examine the bill and check that components which have been charged for have all been fitted.

Firstly, the oil filter housing (a replaceable cartridge on later cars) should be very clean – if it remains covered in oil and dirt then the chances are that the oil filter has not been replaced. The oil on the dipstick should be fairly clear and light in colour – unlike the blackened goo which often clings to dipsticks.

Still on the subject of oil and lubrication, check that the dashpot oil level has been topped up and that the grease nipples on the front suspension are clean (if they are covered with dirt, then the front suspension has not been lubricated, and the kingpins will wear rapidly and could seize as a result).

With regard to the ignition, if the service should include replacement sparking plugs, leads, distributor cap or coil, then do check that they have been replaced. Marking the old components (typist's correction fluid or paint will do) helps in this.

The most frequently charged-for but not fitted components are brake shoes and pads – in fact, this practice was at one time widespread and, as a precaution against the customer asking awkward questions, some mechanics kept an old set of brake shoes handy to show to prying customers. It is, of course, not too difficult

A fine line across the spinner and hub will enable you to tell whether a wheel has been removed during a service and hence whether the brake shoes were checked or renewed – it being very unlikely that the wheel would be re-fitted in exactly the same orientation (spline to spline) and the spinner tightened to the same point!

nor time-consuming a task to remove a wheel to check brake pad thickness, nor a drum to check shoes, but there are precautions which can show up such fraud without you having to get your hands dirty.

For wire wheels: make a discreet mark on the spinner and the wheel using a fine indelible pen. It is very unlikely that the wheel would be re-fitted in the same orientation or that the spinner would be tightened to exactly the same point if the wheel were removed and re-fitted, so if the two marks align perfectly after the service has been carried out, then the chances are that the wheel has remained in situ throughout and the brake shoes were not replaced. Secondly, if you remove one rear road wheel and place typist's correction fluid on the exposed portion of the brake drum stud threads, removal of the brake drum will in turn remove this. If the dried fluid is undisturbed after the service, you know that the drums have not been removed.

For steel/alloy wheels: place typist's correction fluid on the wheelnut studs.

There is no guarantee that you can catch out every little dodge which has been employed by the murkier elements of the trade; obtaining a good workshop manual does, however, tell you exactly which jobs should be carried out and give you a fighting chance of uncovering attempts to rip you off. Best of all, have the servicing carried out by an MGB specialist who has a hard-earned reputation not to be jeopardised by shoddy workmanship or practices.

ADVANCED DIY SERVICING

The 3,000, 6,000 and 12,000 mile (or 3, 6 and 12 monthly intervals – whichever comes sooner) services do require certain specialised equipment but are essentially not too difficult and should pose no insurmountable problems for the average DIY enthusiast.

Each task is given a maximum interval or mileage before it becomes necessary; you can carry them out more frequently if you wish.

VARIOUS (3 MONTHLY) If the water pump is fitted with a grease nipple, apply grease. Oil the door hinges and the door lock mechanisms. Apply oil to the dynamo via the small hole at the rear of the unit.

ENGINE OIL CHANGE (3 MONTHLY HIGH MILEAGE – 6 MONTHLY MAXIMUM) The engine oil and filter should be renewed together. Many people warm the engine before draining the oil, on the basis that this makes the oil thinner and helps it to drain; however, if the engine has been standing idle for some time (perhaps overnight) then the oil will have had sufficient time to drain back into the sump, and running the engine will only serve to redistribute it back around the engine.

Firstly, drain the old oil by removing the sump plug, with a suitable receptacle underneath (an old 5 litre oil can with one side cut away is ideal). The author also unbolts the oil cooler and ties this to the bonnet catch in order to drain as much oil as possible from it. Then turn your attention to the filter. Early MGBs are fitted with canisters which hold a replaceable element (the earliest ones point downwards and are a pain to work with, on later cars the canisters point upwards), and later cars use a disposable filter cartridge. Apply a little clean engine oil to the rubber sealing ring(s) before fitting the canister or cartridge and, if it points downwards when fitted, fill it with fresh engine oil before re-fitting it. Adapter kits are available for early cars which invert the filter housing; if you do your own servicing they are worth fitting.

The author makes a practice of removing the sparking plugs (also the plug leads and distributor cap) and spinning the engine on the starter motor for ten to fifteen seconds in order to get oil pumping around the engine (watch the oil pressure gauge and stop turning the engine over when it registers pressure) before fitting the plugs and firing it up.

IGNITION (6 MONTHLY) Examine all high and low tension ignition wiring for signs of damage, and renew if necessary. A small quantity of oil should be applied to the felt within the distributor drive shaft under the rotor arm, and a few drops should be applied to the mechanical advance mechanism through the base plate. Check the condition of the contact breaker points, renew if necessary (and it is as well to also renew the condenser, because it is this which is the most likely culprit for eroded points contact surfaces) and re-set the gap as already described. The ignition timing should be checked annually or whenever the contact breaker points gap has been altered.

Dynamic timing is far better than static timing but in order to set the timing dynamically you require a stroboscopic light – these are not expensive and available at motor factors.

STATIC TIMING Remove the sparking plugs so that the engine can be turned over until number one cylinder (nearest the radiator) is on its compression stroke. Preferably, remove the rocker box cover so that you can see when both valves of number one cylinder are closed (both rocker arms will be loose) and both rocker arms on number four cylinder are fully depressed; alternatively (and less satisfactorily), you can hold a finger over the spark plug hole of number one cylinder and feel when compression is taking place.

Turn the engine until the timing notch on the crank pulley aligns with the appropriate timing mark, at which precise point, the contact breaker points should be just starting to open. You can check this by eye, or more precisely by switching on the ignition for a few seconds with a 12v bulb connected across the points (it will light the moment the points separate).

To adjust the timing, the distributor body must be turned; slacken the bolt on the base clamp and turn the distributor body until the points separate at the correct time, then re-tighten the bolt. Fine adjustment can be carried out using the vernier adjuster. Turn the crankshaft through a complete revolution and check that the points open at the correct moment.

Finally test drive the car; if the engine pinks under hard acceleration from around thirty mph in fourth gear, retard the ignition timing slightly.

43

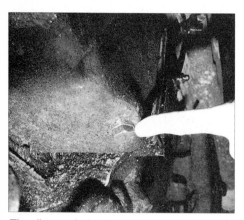

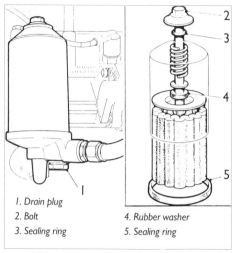

1. Drain plug
2. Bolt
3. Sealing ring
4. Rubber washer
5. Sealing ring

The oil sump drain plug. Always check on the state of the washer and replace it if it is at all damaged. A 5 litre oil container with a side cut out makes a good receptacle for drained oil. Use disposable gloves when removing or refitting the oil drain plug – oil is not kind to your hands!

Mk. 1 MGB owners can obtain a filter head which inverts the filter body. Makes life much easier, and to return the car to original condition you only have to unbolt it again. (Courtesy Autodata).

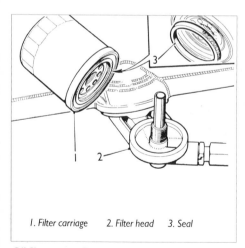

1. Filter carriage   2. Filter head   3. Seal

Oil filter types. Disposable oil filters make life easier. Place a rag under the filter head when removing it to catch the inevitable escaping oil. (Courtesy Autodata).

Oil radiator lifted. For a thorough oil change, unbolt the oil cooler and tie it to the raised bonnet catch. After replenishing the engine oil, I always remove the plugs, leads and distributor cap, then spin the engine on the starter motor to get oil pressure up before re-fitting the plugs and leads and starting the engine.

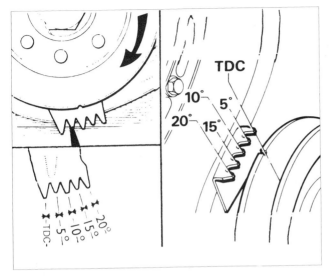

Timing marks. The timing marks of (left) early cars – showing the direction of crank wheel rotation and (right) later cars. (Courtesy Autodata).

Vernier adjuster. Fine adjustments are made with the vernier adjuster, which has arrows to indicate advance and retard.

DYNAMIC TIMING Use typists' correction fluid or a small dab of white paint (allow this to dry before starting the engine) to highlight the timing marks. disconnect and plug the end of the vacuum advance pipe which runs from the inlet manifold. Connect one stroboscope lead to number one spark plug (nearest the radiator) and the other to its high tension lead. Make sure that the stroboscope leads cannot foul the fan blades or generator drive belt, point the timing light at the timing marks and ask an assistant to start the engine, which should previously have been warmed to normal running temperature so that it ticks over smoothly without the choke.

Every time that number one spark plug fires, the stroboscopic light flashes, appearing to arrest the movement of the crankshaft pulley

Strobes and leads. Small stroboscopic lights are quite cheap to buy,
and will repay their cost many times
over. Some, however, give out insufficient light to be seen in normal
daylight conditions, so take advice
when choosing one.

Most especially on cars with
mechanically driven fans, ensure
that the strobe leads cannot
become entangled with moving
parts. Don't forget that around
25,000 volts are coursing through
them every time No.1 spark plug
fires.

timing notch. If the notch is not aligned with
the timing mark, then stop the engine and
rotate the distributor body as already described.

The distributor rotor arm runs anti-clockwise; turn it clockwise to advance the timing
and vice versa, although if only a small adjustment is needed then use the vernier adjuster.
When the timing is correct, ask your assistant
to rev the engine a little, and you should see a
small advance in the timing, caused by the
mechanical advance mechanism – if not, then

the distributor requires attention. Reconnect
the vacuum advance pipe and you should see a
further advance.

DWELL ANGLE (ANNUALLY) The dwell
angle is a measurement which shows how long
the contact breaker points are closed in
between being opened by the cam lobes. While
the points are closed, an electrical charge builds
up in the ignition coil (see Chapter Four) and,
if the points are not in the closed position for

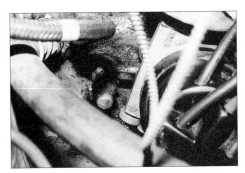

The author prefers to turn the engine off before plunging his arm down through this tangle to get at the vernier adjuster. Any one of the HT leads could give you a belt if you touch it.

Air filter removal – undoing the bolts. Removing the front air filter with a ¹/2" ring spanner. Ring spanners are less prone to slipping off nuts and bolt heads; use them in preference to open-enders when working in the engine bay, to minimise the chances of scraping paint off panels.

Air filter removal. The bracket into which these bolts run also holds the choke cable outer end. Don't lose the small gaskets.

Marking the dashpot. Mark a line across the dashpot and carb body before removing the dashpot.

long enough, this can be too weak and result in a weak spark at the sparking plugs. This causes – amongst other things – engine cold starting problems.

Some automotive multi meters can measure dwell angle, but if you don't have access to one of these then any MOT testing station can carry out the measurement for you. If, after carrying out necessary adjustments to obtain the correct dwell angle, the resultant contact breaker points gap is too small, the cause is

most probably a worn distributor, which will have to be overhauled or replaced.

CARBURATION (6 MONTHLY) There are some compelling reasons for having the carburettors checked, balanced and the mixture set professionally rather than tackling it yourself. Apart from the obvious increase in fuel consumption which comes from mal-adjusted or faulty carburettors, engine wear will increase alarmingly if the mixture is too rich or too lean. Furthermore, some problems such as air induction which might allow you to set the mixture correctly with the engine at tickover will be manifest only when the engine is revved. Without exhaust gas analysing equipment, you have no means to objectively judge the effects of any adjustments you do make.

You can balance the carburettors and roughly set the mixture without specialist equipment, but it is recommended that you do so only when it is necessary in order to get the car running well enough to make it to an MOT test centre or garage which does have ignition and exhaust analysis equipment.

CHECKING THE NEEDLE AND JET

(ANNUALLY) Remove the dashpots, noting how each fits because they must go back on in exactly the same orientations. Carefully lift out the piston from each carb, and examine the needle. If there is a wear ridge on it then it should be replaced, along with the jet. Examine the jet; if is appears the slightest bit oval then it and the needle should be replaced and the jet centred. This work is covered in all workshop manuals and also in *MGB Restoration/ Preparation/ Maintenance.*

BALANCING THE CARBURETTORS

(6 MONTHLY) The engine should be warmed to normal operating temperature so that it ticks over without choke. Remove the air filters. Disconnect the choke cable. Slacken one nut on the throttle linkage so that the carbs can operate independently of each other.

Start the engine and, using a length of rubber or plastic pipe with one end held to your ear and the other in the carburettor throats, listen to the rush of air into each carburettor. If one is drawing more air than the other, adjust one

Spanner on carb linkage nut. In order to balance the two carburettors, one linkage nut must firstly be slackened so that the two can operate independently of each other.

Balancing carbs with a rubber pipe. Use a length of rubber pipe or garden hose to listen to the rush of air into the carb throat; when it sounds the same from each carb, the two are balanced. When pinching up the linkage nut, ensure that both forks act simultaneously.

of the idle screws until the rush of air into each carb sounds the same. Re-tighten the linkage clamp nut. DIY carburettor balancing kits which actually measure the amount of air drawn in are fairly inexpensive and will give more accurate results.

SETTING THE MIXTURE (6 MONTHLY) The

ignition timing must be spot-on and all elements of the ignition and carburation should

Adjusting the mixture. To enrich the mixture (HS4 carburettors), wind the nut clockwise (viewed from above) – vice versa to make it leaner. On the HIF carburettor, there is a screw for mixture adjustment (see text).

Carb throat showing the jet. If you manually lift the piston, you will be able to see the jet. If you're setting the mixture from scratch, raise this so that it is level with the bridge, then (HS4) wind it back down twelve flats (three complete turns), and proceed from there, or (HIF) turn the adjusting screw anticlockwise until the jet is level with the bridge, clockwise until the jet starts to move, then two full turns clockwise.

Adjusting the idle screw. When the mixture has been set, adjust the idle screws by equal amounts until the desired tickover is reached. (Front air filter removed for photographic purposes only – set tickover with both filters in situ.)

You need only a small screwdriver, a ⅜" (8mm) open-end spanner and some tube to balance the carbs. I've seen a professional mechanic set the mixture without firstly balancing the carbs – if you have the mixture set professionally, it is worth balancing the carbs beforehand, just in case.

Gunson Gas tester. If you want to do the job without any fear of inaccuracy, beg or borrow one of these or, alternatively, take the car to an MOT testing station and have the work carried out there.

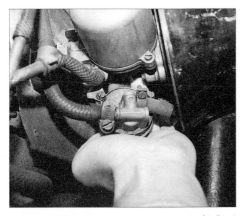

Lifting pin. The lifting pin raises the piston by $^1/_{32}$" – if the revolutions die away when this happens the mixture is too lean; if the revs rise it's too rich. When the mixture is right the revs should rise almost imperceptibly and then return to normal. For the best in fuel economy, however, exhaust gas testing equipment should be used.

be in good order. The valve clearances should also be correct.

The advice given here is intended only to get the engine running well enough for the car to be driven to a service centre which has exhaust analysing equipment. With SU HS4 (separate float chamber) units, to make the mixture richer, the jet must be lowered, which is accomplished by unscrewing the nut at the bottom of the carburettor one flat at a time, and vice-versa to make the mixture more lean. Begin by removing the air filters, and adjusting both jet nuts so that the jets can be seen to be flush with the jet bridges in the carburettor throats; it is necessary to lift the pistons manually in order to see the jet bridges. Unscrew each jet adjusting nut by twelve flats (three complete turns), then re-fit the air filters and test run the engine.

Adjust both idle screws by equal amounts to set the tickover, then adjust the jet adjusting nuts by equal amounts (no more than one flat

at a time) until the fastest tickover is achieved, and finally re-adjust the idle screws.

The HIF carburettors fitted to later cars are more sophisticated units, with separate choke jets and having the main jet held by a bi-metallic bracket which varies the mixture according to temperature. The mixture is altered by turning a screw in the main carburettor body under the fuel inlet; it is screwed in to enrich the mixture, out to make it leaner. If starting from scratch, lift the piston so that you can see the jet bridge, and turn the screw out (anti-clockwise) until the jet is level with the bridge. Turn the screw in (clockwise) through two complete turns, then check and adjust further as may be necessary, following the principles as already described.

STEERING/SUSPENSION (6 MONTHLY)

Check the steering rack gaiters for oil leakage, and apply grease via the steering rack grease nipple (where fitted). Check the dampers for fluid leakage. Grease the kingpins.

VALVE CLEARANCES (6 MONTHLY)

Remove the rocker box cover, taking care not to damage the cork oil seal unless this is to be replaced. Remove the sparking plugs. The engine has to be turned over, which can be accomplished in several alternative ways. You can (car our of gear) pull on the fan belt, use a 1 $^5/_{16}$" socket and ratchet on the crankshaft pulley nut, place the car in 4th gear and push it backwards and forwards or place the car in 4th gear, raise one rear wheel and have an accomplice to turn this.

Turn the engine until valve number 8 is fully open, that is, the stem of the rearmost valve has been depressed to its maximum by the rocker. When valve 8 is fully open then the gap at valve 1 (nearest the radiator) should be set. Note that the sum of the valve numbers is 8+1 (9); this is generally referred to as the 'Rule of Nine'. The sum of the valve to be checked and that which is fully open always equals nine with

Rocker box cover. Take care not to damage the cork gasket when lifting the rocker box cover. The state of the oil around the valve gear can tell you quite a lot about the engine. If there is a yellow-ochre gunge this can be caused by too many short journeys, or by water entering the oil via the cylinder head gasket or a cracked head or block – certainly it deserves investigation. If you find traces of burnt material then one of the valve stems, guides or seals is probably damaged and most certainly in need of attention.

Valve gap adjustment. Use a parallel-bladed screwdriver to hold the rocker adjusting screw while you slacken the nut using a $^1/2''$ ring spanner. Don't use a tapered blade screwdriver, because this opens the slot up and makes accurate setting more difficult in future. Holding the adjuster perfectly still whilst you pinch up the locking nut can take a bit of practice. Re-check the clearance and keep on adjusting it until you learn to do it properly.

When re-fitting the rocker box cover, take care to position the cork gasket correctly.

Air filter re-fit. Juggling the brackets whilst not losing the gaskets and getting the bolts started might be a little awkward the first time you come to re-fit the air filters, but you soon get the hang of it.

the B series four cylinder engine. Turn the engine until valve 6 is open, and check valve 3. The remaining sequence is (first number signifies open valve, second number is valve to be adjusted) 4+5, 7+2, 1+8, 3+6, 5+4, 2+7.

To adjust a valve if the clearance is not as recommended in the specifications, lock the ball end screw using a screwdriver and loosen the locknut with a $^{1}/2$" ring spanner. With the feeler gauge in position, gently tighten the adjuster until the gauge can be moved and offers just a little resistance, and then hold the adjuster still with the screwdriver while you tighten the locknut and finally re-check the gap.

Special tools are available which make carrying out this task a little easier, though the infrequency with which you have to adjust valve clearances makes them rather a luxury item!

UNDER THE CAR (6 MONTHLY) The handbrake cable cover should be fitted with a grease nipple; apply grease until clean grease emerges from the end.

The propeller shaft is fitted with a grease nipple and, in some cases, the spider also has one. Chock the front wheels and place the car in neutral gear. Raise one side of the car and support it using axle stands. Turn the raised

rear wheel until the grease nipple(s) become visible, then pump in clean grease.

Check the brake shoes and pads for wear. Slacken the wheel nuts or spinners on the rear wheels, chock the front wheels, raise the rear of the car and support it on axle stands. Remove the road wheels. Apply the handbrake and remove the brake drum nuts, disengage the handbrake, back off the brake adjusters and pull the drums off. It may prove necessary to sharply tap the brake drum with a soft-faced mallet to centre the shoes. If the friction material thickness is approaching $^{1}/32$" (bonded) or is getting close to the rivets then replace the shoes as a set, both sides of the car. Re-adjust the handbrake.

To check the brake pads, slacken the wheelnuts or spinners, chock the rear wheels, raise the front of the car and support it on axle stands. Remove the road wheels.

Remove the two split pins at the rear of the calliper, along with the pad retaining clips. It should now be possible to remove the pads. The accepted minimum pad friction material is $^{1}/16$", but the author would strongly recommend replacing the pads long before they became this thin – not only for safety reasons but also because the longer the calliper pistons

53

Greasing prop shaft. If one rear wheel is raised from the ground and turned, this will rotate the propeller shaft so that the grease nipple(s) can be reached.

Below: **Brake shoes in situ.** An exploded view of the rear brakes. (Courtesy Autodata).

1. Backplate
2. Backplate to axle case bolt
3. Nut
4. Spring washer
5. Shoe assembly
6. Pull-off spring – cylinder end
7. Pull-off spring – adjustment end
8. Brake shoe steady pin
9. Brake shoe steady spring
10. Retainer washer
11. Adjuster assembly
12. Tappet
13. Wedge
    spindle
14. Adjuster to backplate nut
15. Spring washer

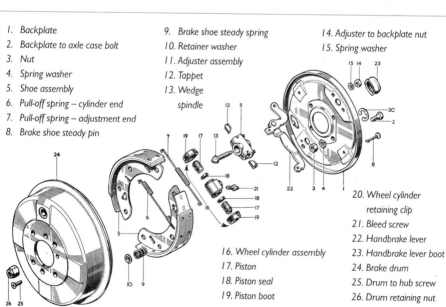

16. Wheel cylinder assembly
17. Piston
18. Piston seal
19. Piston boot
20. Wheel cylinder
    retaining clip
21. Bleed screw
22. Handbrake lever
23. Handbrake lever boot
24. Brake drum
25. Drum to hub screw
26. Drum retaining nut

Removing brake shoes. This is the author's wire wheeled car. Begin the brake strip by slackening the spinners or nuts, raising the rear of the car, removing the wheelnuts (handbrake engaged) then disengage the handbrake.

Slacken the brake adjuster.

It may prove necessary to give the brake drum a few hefty clouts with the copper faced mallet before the shoes are centred and the drum can be pulled away.

Don't breathe in brake dust. Empty
the drum out of doors and vacuum
the rest from the backplate.

Remove the shoe locators. Hold
the pin steady at the rear of the
backplate, grasp the disc with pliers,
and push and twist it.

Then repeat the process for the
other locator. This (and re-fitting
them) may seem a fiddle at first but,
once you've done it a few times it
becomes second nature.

Make a mental note of which way around the shoes and springs fit before stripping the assembly further.

Ease the top of one shoe out of the adjuster tappet fork, then do the same with the top of the other shoe. If you only intend removing the adjuster mechanism to free it then you need go no further with these instructions.

To remove the brake shoes, remove the top spring then ease the bottoms of the shoes out of the wheel cylinder tappet forks, remove the lower spring and manoeuvre each shoe off the handbrake lever assembly. It is a good precaution to place a strong elastic band around the wheel cylinder assembly to hold the tappets in position – if they come out you'll lose fluid. Reassembly – as malicious DIY mechanical repair manuals always say – is the opposite of stripping; in this case it happens to be true!

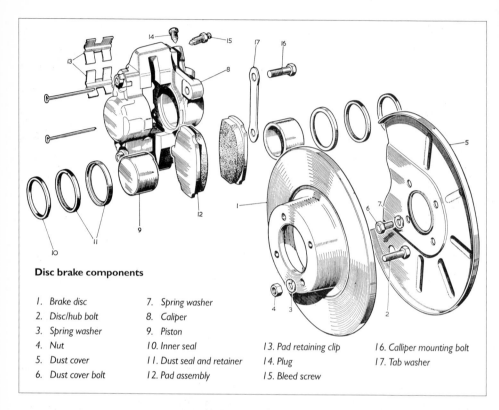

Disc brake components

1. Brake disc
2. Disc/hub bolt
3. Spring washer
4. Nut
5. Dust cover
6. Dust cover bolt
7. Spring washer
8. Caliper
9. Piston
10. Inner seal
11. Dust seal and retainer
12. Pad assembly
13. Pad retaining clip
14. Plug
15. Bleed screw
16. Calliper mounting bolt
17. Tab washer

Above: Removing brake pads is easy. Remove the split pin pad retainers and their clips, then pull the pads out. You may need to use a mole grip. (Courtesy Autodata)

Right: **Pushing the calliper pistons.** You can buy special tools for returning pistons into the calliper. Small G clamps can work, but this is equally effective. One adjustable spanner and a length of steel bar. Don't allow the piston to tip in the bore, as this will damage the seals. Always keep the other piston in place by fitting a pad of appropriate thickness or using a small G clamp.

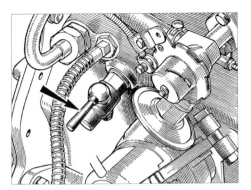

Draining coolant. If you are in the habit of laying your MGB up for the winter months, you can drain the block of coolant completely – provided that the tap is not seized solid. Sadly, most seem to be, so either replace them or use a 50% anti-freeze mixture. (Courtesy Autodata).

Starter solenoid connections. The two wires – one brown, one white/red – from the starter solenoid are not fused. Inspect both regularly for signs of damage.

are left exposed the greater the chances of their corroding.

To push the pistons back into the callipers in order to fit new pads, clamp one piston using a small G clamp or refit the original pad, then place a steel strip $1/8$" x 1" x 6" (all sizes approximate) in the calliper so that one edge bears against the centreline of a piston and the other the disc. Use an adjustable spanner to turn the steel strip, and the piston will be forced back into the calliper. Special tools are available for this.

ENGINE BAY GENERAL (ANNUALLY) Each air filter casing is held by two bolts; remove these and pull the air filter casings clear. Renew the air filter elements and sealing rings. If fitted, renew the in-line fuel filter. Check the crankcase breather pipes and clean them out if necessary.

Renew the contact breaker points, the condenser, the sparking plugs and – if you like – the distributor cap, high tension leads, low tension lead (25D distributor only) and the coil. Note that some later cars (and V8s) are fitted

Bleeding the brake system at a wheel cylinder. Rather than use the traditional jam jar with brake fluid inside the author drilled a hole in the plastic cap of an old brake fluid container – and ended a personal tradition of spilling brake fluid from said jam jars! The pipe is a fairly tight fit in the hole so that, even if this gets knocked over, it does not leak. By hooking the pipe over the rear leaf spring, the author ensures that the length of rising pipe constantly holds fluid above the bleed nipple, so there is no need to ensure that the pipe end is actually immersed in fluid. Open the bleed nipple, get an accomplice to press the brake pedal down and hold it down while you re-tighten the nipple, and repeat these steps until pure fluid with no air bubbles emerges from the nipple.

59

with a 6V coil and a ballast resistor; make sure that you obtain the right one! Most if not all of these items can be bought in 'ignition service kit' form at lower than their combined individual prices and, if you choose to buy them as a set then it makes sense to fit them as a set.

ENGINE BAY (EVERY TWO YEARS) Renew the fanbelt. Slacken the generator bolts then push the generator towards the engine so that the fan belt can be removed. After fitting the new belt, re-tension it as already described. Renew the antifreeze. If you did not do so as part of an earlier service, renew the distributor cap and high tension leads.

It is a good precaution to renew the various cooling system hoses – if not, examine them and replace any which show signs of ageing. Check all wiring for signs of damage.

UNDER THE CAR (EVERY TWO YEARS) Renew the gearbox and axle oil. Check the wheel bearings; replace if necessary and repack with grease – work best left to professionals.

(EVERY THREE YEARS) Renew the brake flexible hoses. Renew the brake and clutch hydraulic fluid – replace it with silicone fluid and you won't ever have to replace it again!

ECONOMY

In the modern conservation-minded world, some motor manufacturers have made reasonable advances in the fuel economy of their cars and, judged against such cars, the MGB has unfortunately high fuel consumption. Before looking at this subject in depth, it is worth pointing out that the MGB is one of the most ecologically sound cars of all, despite its high fuel usage, because a major part (40% in fact) of the total pollution caused by a vehicle occurs during its manufacture, so that a vehicle like the MGB which typically lasts twice as long as most other cars (if not even longer) could

actually cause less pollution overall! In practice, the average fuel consumption appears to be around one gallon every 25-27 miles, although many owners fail to achieve this and waste fuel through not having their cars set up correctly.

The key to fuel economy is really no more than having everything working efficiently, and this means having the ignition set spot-on and with no unnecessary electrical losses which can reduce the power of the spark, then correctly setting up the carburation. It is possible to set carburation fairly accurately at home using simple tools, but the twin carburettor set up of the MGB really demands that specialised equipment be used to firstly balance and 'needle' (find and fit the most appropriate needle to) the carburettors, then to set the mixture of fuel and air accurately.

In order to accurately adjudge the effects of alterations to the mixture, it is necessary to use an exhaust gas analyser. These tell the technician exactly what comes out of the exhaust pipe and, from this information he can then adjust the mixture settings until the optimum amount of fuel is being delivered into the cylinders. Nowadays, these analysers are often built into ignition analysis machines, such as those manufactured by Crypton and Sun, and which are found at most service centres. In the UK, Ministry Of Transport (MOT) vehicle testing stations must now possess such equipment.

Even better results can be obtained by combining an exhaust gas analyser with a rolling road, which is a device for measuring the power output by a car at the driving wheels. Such machines are found at performance car preparation businesses and, although having the mixture set here will cost far more than having it done at an MOT station, you can have the car set up to give a combination of satisfactory performance coupled with the desired fuel economy. Be warned, however, that this type of professional equipment can highlight faults with items such as a sticking or badly worn (and in need of replacement) distributor or its drive gear, or worn carburettors which require at best new dashpots and pistons and at worst complete replacement. Your 'economy drive' could prove to be very expensive!

The alternative is to set the carburation yourself at home by following a number of steps and using very rough testing methods to find the best mixture, or to utilise one of a number of commercially available products which help you to more accurately set the mixture. DIY engine tuning should only be attempted by experienced persons, because there are any number of faults which can have a fundamental effect on fuel economy, but which will not be apparent to the novice, and which may be made apparent by any of the commercially available tuning devices. These can include a weak spark, worn distributor or drive, air induction and a multitude of carburation problems.

As an illustration of the type of fault which can only usually be found by using specialised equipment, a worn distributor can, with the contact breaker points gap set correctly, give too small a 'dwell' angle – that is, the amount of time which the points are closed before the next cam lobe opens them. This does not give the coil primary winding sufficient time to build up a satisfactory charge, and results in a weak spark at the plugs, which normally makes its presence felt during cold starting, at which time, the enriched air/fuel mixture needs a good strong spark to ignite it.

There is no substitute for exhaust gas measuring and ignition testing equipment and a lot of operator experience. The low-cost DIY exhaust gas testers which have quite recently become available are in the experience of the author quite accurate enough for the purpose and are highly recommended. You can find advice on how to set carburation in most good workshop manuals and in *MGB – Restoration/Preparation/Maintenance* by the same author and published by Osprey Automotive.

Many people are taking advantage of the cost savings offered by unleaded fuel in most countries today, and although unleaded fuel should NEVER be used in the standard MGB it is possible to use unleaded fuel in the car PROVIDED that the cylinder head is firstly replaced with a more suitable modified version. These are now widely advertised and are available as exchange items; that is, you fit the new cylinder head then send the old one away to the company concerned. A substantial deposit, refundable on receipt of your old cylinder head, will be levied. Before switching to an unleaded-compatible cylinder head in the interests of reducing pollution, reflect that unleaded fuel gives worse emissions than leaded UNLESS it is used in conjunction with a catalytic converter. Worse, 'cats' only operate when they have reached a high operating temperature, so that a modern cat equipped car burning unleaded fuel but used predominantly for short journeys can pump out far more pollution than a properly set-up MGB burning leaded fuel. At the time of writing, no known after-market catalytic converter is available for the MGB – nor is any likely to be made available, unless legislation forces it.

A cylinder head suitable for use with unleaded fuel is an expensive item, and to recoup the costs in lower fuel bills could take a period of some years! The difference in cost between a modified exchange cylinder head and an ordinary exchange head is not so great, so that if you envisage having to buy an exchange cylinder head, then bear in mind that for comparatively little extra you could opt for the unleaded variety and recoup the extra expense in a relatively short period.

FALSE ECONOMIES

Many gadgets claimed to reduce fuel consumption have been offered to the motorist over the years. At one time, it was possible to add up the percentage fuel savings claimed for the gadgets to over 100% so that, theoretically, if you fitted them all to your own car then far from having to put petrol in your car, the tank would fill from the engine as the car was driven!

The Trades Descriptions Act took care of some of these ridiculous advertising claims in the UK, but they did not do away with the fuel-saving gadget itself. The reason is that the fines imposed on companies which make false advertising claims for such gadgets are far lower than some of the profits to be made from their activities – in other words, they find it profitable to openly flout the law!

It is not possible to state with 100% certainty that none of these devices can improve your fuel economy, but readers are generally advised to spend their money on having their cars' ignition and carburation systems correctly set up and maintained rather than on fuel saving gadgetry. Even if your ignition and carburation were perfectly set up, you can waste fuel if the car's tyre pressures are too low, or worse, if the rear brakes are binding.

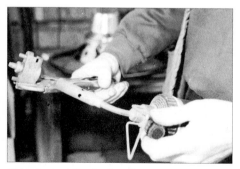

Using heat to free brake adjuster. When you have removed the adjuster mechanism, pull out the tappets, grasp the cylinder using a mole grip or similar and apply heat to the aluminium body. This expands quickly, so try to turn the adjuster every couple of minutes until you get some movement. Allow the unit to cool, then apply freeing liquid to the threads and begin working the adjuster forwards and backwards – a fraction of a turn to begin with but by greater amounts each time – until it can be removed.

Driving with binding brakes is rather like constantly driving up a very steep hill, and the fuel wastage is enormous. It is easy enough to test for binding brakes. Take the car for a short run (using the brakes a little to warm them up), then jack up one corner at a time and spin the wheels by hand. Binding will be obvious. The front disc brakes should drag very slightly when tested in this way, but if real rolling resistance is felt then remedial action will be necessary.

Rear drum brakes are adjustable, and slackening off the adjuster (using the proper tool) by one click may or may not stop the binding. If not, the brake assembly will have to be stripped, freed and properly lubricated. If you have never undertaken this type of work before then either consult a good workshop manual before proceeding or have the work carried out professionally.

Binding of the front brakes is caused by sticking pistons within the callipers. Exchange calliper units are available, and offer the best option for the DIY enthusiast, although it is by no means impossible to service the callipers at home (consult a good workshop manual). Preferably, the work should be undertaken professionally.

Binding brakes can also be caused by problems with the master cylinder, or damaged brake lines – consult professionals if you have such problems.

Having too-low tyre pressures will not only increase fuel consumption, but it will also accelerate tyre wear.

Do not be tempted to over-inflate the tyres to compensate, however, because this will also accelerate tyre wear but more importantly it will reduce the road-holding of the car in certain circumstances.

While on the subject of tyres, the greatest cost saving you can make is not to get caught with illegal ones! In the UK, the fine *per illegal tyre* is enough to buy a complete new set of high quality tyres.

ECONOMY DRIVE

One of the greatest aids to fuel economy is a light accelerator foot! How you drive the car has a huge bearing on miles per gallon. If you go all out for speed between the bends and brake frequently, then you can expect maximum fuel consumption.

Driving economically, however, does not necessarily mean driving slowly. It takes a great amount of energy to accelerate a car to a fixed speed, and equally as much energy to stop it from that speed! Every time you apply the brakes, you are wasting energy (in the form of burnt mixture) which would otherwise help maintain your forward momentum. So the less you can use the brakes the better (this also saves on brake wear).

Reducing use of the brakes is easier and not as dangerous as it may at first sound. The secret is to do what any good driver should and to look and think ahead at all times. Instead of braking immediately before reaching a corner, try to slowly decelerate so that the car is travelling at the correct speed when you reach it, and treat obstacles in the road, such as parked vehicles which have to be passed, in the same way. Reducing acceleration and building up speed slowly instead can also save a lot of fuel, because cars drink petrol very quickly when the throttle is fully open. In both acceleration and braking, the accent is on driving the car as smoothly and gently as possible and consistent with road safety.

On long, straight roads, you can save much fuel by reducing your speed to an optimum level consistent with available travelling time and road safety. Those who have driven cars with accurate fuel flow (MGP) meters on motorways will be aware that fuel consumption per mile travelled increases alarmingly along with speed. The exact speeds at which consumption increases will vary according to the type of car, whether it has overdrive etc, but basically, remember that sixty miles per hour is

cheaper than seventy, but more expensive than fifty-five! In the case of busy motorways, however, the advantages of fuel saving are outweighed by the safety factor in keeping pace with the other traffic.

To illustrate what can be achieved by more careful driving, the author managed to obtain 28.8 mpg from his 1966 GT, which usually returns a consistent 25mpg. At 1994 prices, this would save about £60 worth of petrol per 5,000 miles travelled.

One last word on this subject. After fitting a new wiring loom, the author discovered that the fuel consumption dropped to one gallon per 29.8 miles, even when the car was driven fairly hard over predominantly short journeys. The only explanation can be that faulty wiring in the ignition circuit was giving the coil insufficient charge, resulting in a weak spark. Low cost devices which check the strength of the spark are available from the MGOC and most motor factors – one of these would make a sound investment.

OTHER ECONOMIES

There is far more to the subject of economical motoring than pure miles per gallon, and while in the fuel economy department the MGB might fare badly in comparison with more recent cars, in other respects it places the modern car a very poor second. The prices of MGB spares are generally very low in comparison with most modern cars and, what is more, those spares are normally easier to obtain. The simple technology of the MGB keeps professional mechanical repairs costs low, and permits owner-servicing, which is not always feasible with today's electronics-dependent vehicles.

It is in the area of depreciation that the MGB shows the greatest economies in comparison with modern cars. At the time of writing, the depreciation of the modern car has never been at a more frightening level, and some up-market executive cars are depreciating in a year or two

Cleaning upholstery. You can obtain special vinyl/leather cleaners – use these with an old toothbrush to scrub out dirt contained in the surface grain.

by enough to fund an MGB restoration! MGBs are not currently depreciating – neither are they appreciating and, while no-one can predict with confidence future trends in classic and modern car depreciation, it is difficult to imagine any great change in the foreseeable future.

LOOKING AFTER YOUR BODY

The vast majority of surviving MGBs nowadays either have body rot or have had body rot which has been made good by the use of repair or replacement panels or – sadly – which has been camouflaged with various body fillers. There is no need for a car body to deteriorate in this manner if it is properly looked after.

General bodywork maintenance comprises regularly washing the car and waxing the paintwork so that it repels water – modern car shampoos both wash and wax at the same time and are recommended. Before washing the paintwork, however, clean mud from within the wheelarches and from the castle rails using a garden hose and preferably a stiff broom head. If the paintwork is dull, it can usually be lightly cut back (T-Cut or similar) and polished to a shine. Modern colour-enriched polishes appear in the experience of the author to work well, disguising small scratches, as well as any

scroll marks made during paint preparation.

The MGB bodyshell is manufactured from steel which, if it is allowed to come into contact with moist air, will quickly rust – that is, the surface will oxidise. In order to prevent this, manufacturers place various coatings on car bodyshells; some are galvanised (given a coating of zinc which is very tough and which bonds to the steel), but most make do with paint. If bright steel is painted then it should not rust, but when the paintwork is breached, watch out!

Any small scratches which go right through to bright steel should be remedied at the earliest opportunity – even painting on a touch of primer using a small artist's brush will afford some protection until the repair can be attended to properly. Very small scratches can sometimes be topcoated in the same way – brush on three or four coats (cellulose – a couple of coats will do with synthetic paint) of topcoat, allow this to harden – preferably for six weeks – then use a proprietary cutting compound on the repair and the surrounding area.

Larger scratches should have their edges 'feathered'; that is, the hard shoulder should be gently sanded out. Then primer can be applied by brush or spray, followed by topcoats.

PLASTIC PROTECTION

There are two accessories which can, in the long-term, help protect your car's bodywork. Mud flaps protect the castle rail front end and the rear side bodywork from constant dousing in muddy – often salted during the winter months – water. These are easily fitted using self-tapping screws but themselves form small rust-traps of a kind, so drill the mounting holes and douse the area of bodywork which will be covered by the mudflap top ends with a wax-based product such as Waxoyl or Dinitrol before fitting the flaps.

In recent years, moulded under-wing protectors have become available for the B and these are an excellent idea *provided* that they are fitted only over sound, rust-free steel. The author would recommend taking the areas to be covered by the undershields back to bare metal then giving them plenty of paint and also wax protection before the shields are fitted.

SURVIVING IN YOUR MGB

Although the MGB was at its launch the most comfortable MG sports car yet made, and despite the fact that the car was constantly refined during its production life to the point at which it resembled (an admittedly cramped) luxury car inside rather than a typically austere 1960s sports car in its dotage, there is much which can be done to improve creature comforts. However, there are also many ways to fritter away money on questionable and sometimes pointless modifications.

Any car which has been around as long as the MGB and which exists in such quantities as the MGB will be viewed as fair game by manufacturers of accessories. Some accessories give worthwhile improvements in performance, safety or comfort, but there are many accessories whose only value is ornamental. The decision whether to fit either worthy or flippant accessories rests with the owner.

Those who own early and original or historically important MGBs (perhaps with an eye to the market value of the cars) may not wish to fit any non-original accessories, preferring to keep their cars as 'authentic' as possible, and many owners of more commonplace vintages believe that any accessory which is out of period will detract from the correctness of their cars. In addition, a major part of the pleasure which comes from owning an MGB is that which you gain from driving an authentic period car with all its attendant period shortcomings! However, for every purist who views his or her MGB as some sort of shrine which is never to be contaminated by modern gadgetry, there will be a number who wish to personalise or improve their cars by the fitting of accessories.

The majority of accessories sold at your local motor factors are furnished with full and perfectly adequate fitting details, and there really can be no justification for duplicating these in a book. However, certain accessories may prove especially difficult to fit into certain years of MGB, and in such instances extra instruction is certainly valid and will be included in this chapter.

CREATURE COMFORTS

The Mark 1 Roadster and GT seats don't offer very much in the way of padding for the posterior and, coupled with vigorous new suspension springs and dampers, can give the derriere something of a pounding on bumpy roads. There are many after-market competition or just plain luxurious seats which can be adapted to fit or for which you can buy subframes for the MGB floorpans, and you can peruse these at most larger motor factors or in catalogues such as that produced by Ripspeed. Most owners of comparatively rare early Mk.1 cars are probably able and willing to suffer minor discomfort from the original seats in the interests of originality: where the seating support can cause very real problems is in lumber support.

People with back problems (including the author) might like to follow the example of the author and place a folded bath towel between the seat back and the small of their back. With a little adjustment, it can mean the difference between enjoyable motoring and purgatory – especially on long journeys. It's not just Mk.1 MGB seats which are wanting in the lumber support department, and a folded towel or small cushion is a far better solution than taking pain-killing tablets no matter what year your MGB is!

Now comes the (not so) clever bit. Hands up all those MGB owners who, while wearing shorts, have lowered their bare legs onto a leather or vinyl seat base which has been heated to near melting point by strong summer

MGR V8 interior. My, isn't it sumptuous compared to most MG sportscars? The MGOC sell interior trim kits which come as near as dammit to replicating this type of opulence so, if your tastes are more for Aston Martin than Austin Metro, why not take the plunge?

Old leather seats can often be repaired – these are beyond help. Fitted some years ago as a stop gap measure while I tried to find a pair of good original seats in the correct colour, the leather is now brittle and badly torn. After re-spraying the car (see Chapter Three), the seats looked a positive disgrace. Something had to be done.

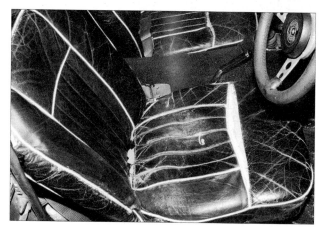

sun (yipe!), hands up all those whose shirt has become wet and sticky all up their back on a long drive in hot weather. OK, unfold your bath towel and drape it down the seat back and over the base. Blissful unsticky motoring is now assured.

Taking this idea a stage further (and high on the author's list of future projects), those with a sewing machine might care to run up a pair of seat covers in non-stretch towelling, incorporating lumber support in the form of a little padding and preferably affixed inside the cover using velcro, so that the support is removable for washing.

Owners of later MGBs are catered for (spoiled for choice?) by the MG Owners' Club and many MG spares specialists, who offer not only standard seat covers but more luxurious alternatives which don't look at all out of place on later cars. With the arrival of the sumptuously appointed MGR V8 no-one can argue that luxurious trim and MGBs don't mix.

These may look like standard Mk.I MGB leather seats, but if you sit in them then the difference becomes crystal clear – they're very comfortable. The seats were hand made by a local upholsterer, Bernie Lewis. Bernie listened to my grumbling about back pain after driving the car, and set about tailoring seats very close to the original pattern but which could incorporate the extra padding and stiffening to alleviate Tyler's troublesome back. If you fancy a unique interior for your MGB, Bernie's your man!

NOISE SUPPRESSION

Some early MGBs have nothing more than rubber mats on the floor, which not only allows a lot of in-cab noise but also does nothing to insulate the interior from heat dissipating from the transmission tunnel and the nearside floor over the exhaust system. Fitting carpets addresses both problems.

Carpets come in three varieties; you can buy carpet in a roll and tailor it yourself, you can buy economy carpet kits which fit where they touch or you can splash out rather more and buy a set of quality carpets, including a moulded section which fits the transmission tunnel.

Relatively few will opt for the complete DIY approach of buying carpet on the roll, because in addition to the difficulties of the tailoring (make paper templates before cutting up carpet), not everyone has access to a machine capable of stitching the edge seams to prevent them from fraying. You'll also need a rubber or carpet 'sacrificial' mat on the driver's side to prevent your shoe heels from wearing through the carpet in next to no time.

Economy carpet sets are pre-cut and usually edge stitched (the better ones will have a moulded heel panel to prevent your shoe heels from wearing through in the space of a few weeks), but won't include either a moulded transmission tunnel carpet (making fitting far more difficult) or sound deadening material. In the experience of the author, four to five years' use is all you'll get before cheap carpets begin to look down at heel.

The best kits are those which do included a moulded transmission tunnel carpet, have toe board carpets ready fixed to board, extra soundproofing material and all fittings. They are expensive, but will out-last cheaper alternatives and will be much easier to fit.

Probably the most awkward part of fitting carpets is locating the seat base mounting holes and the various holes for self-tapping screws which hold trim and accessories. The author uses a fine pointed scribe to poke through the carpet until each hole is located.

Extra sound deadening material is available off the roll or in shaped kits, and is well worth fitting to cut down on mechanical and road noise. Replacing tattered old under-bonnet sound deadening material with new will reduce engine noise – most especially tappet noise – simply glue it into position.

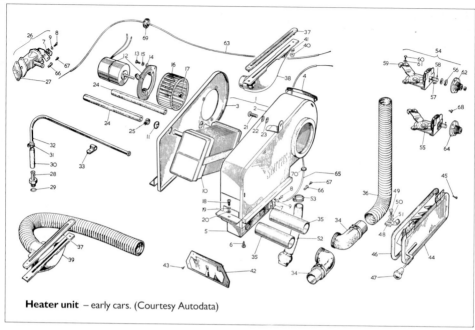

Heater unit – early cars. (Courtesy Autodata)

1. Heater assembly	13. Screw	26. Water valve	38. Demister nozzle	50. Spring	62. Heat control
2. Cover	14. Washer	27. Gasket	39. Demister nozzle	washer	cable
3. Cover slip	15. Spring washer	28. Water union	40. Nut	51. Washer	63. Heat control
4. Cover clip	16. Runner	29. Washer	41. Spring washer	52. Drain tube	cable
5. Outlet duct	17. Collet	30. Hose	42. Heater outlet	53. Tube clip	64. Air knob
6. Screw	18. Screw	31. Hose clip	flap	54. Heat control	65. Air control
7. Cable clamp	19. Washer	32. Return clip	43. Screw	55. Air control	cable
8. Screw	20. Spring washer	33. Inlet manifold clip	44. Fresh air vent	56. Locking nut	66. Trunnion
9. Shakerproof	21. Screw	34. Demister elbow	45. Screw	57. Knob clip	67. Screw
10. Radiator	22. Washer	35. Connector tube	46. Seal	58. Kob pin	68. Rivet
11. Washer	23. Spring clip	36. Demister hose	47. Knob	59. Cable clamp	69. Grommet
12. Motor and	24. Hose	37. Demister	48. Vent spring	60. Screw	70. Grommet
mounting plate	25. Hose clip	escutcheon	49. Screw	61. Sping washer	

HEATER

The heater works by forcing air through a matrix (a small radiator) through which the water pump provides a constant flow of hot engine coolant when the valve on the return pipe – operated by the heater control knob – is open. Its efficiency was never anything to write home about and, when the matrix is old, it can become internally blocked and even less efficient. Before ripping out the heater unit to

replace or flush the matrix, do check that the feed and return pipes and hoses are not blocked, and try disconnecting each (one from the water pump side and the return from the heater control on the offside of the engine block) and pumping water through the system using a garden hose to flush it out. Also, unbolt the valve from the side of the engine block and check that there is no internal restriction – if a previous owner used 'instant gasket' material here then it can melt and in time form a partial diaphragm across the bore. Fit the proper gasket when you replace the valve.

If you require more heat than the standard matrix is capable of furnishing, more efficient units are nowadays available from MGB spares specialists. Fitting these is easy, getting the heater unit out of the car and back in is the problem! Firstly, the five Philips-headed set screws usually have distorted drive slots and have to be drilled out. Lack of clearance for an electric drill means that you can only get a bit onto the screws if you use a flexible drive shaft. The remains of the heads can then be chiselled off if necessary.

On early cars, from inside the car, remove the ashtray, remove the two bolts which run up into the base of the dashboard at the top of the speaker housing and pull the speaker panel out far enough for the speaker wires to be disconnected, then remove the panel. On later cars remove the radio console. Use a stubby screwdriver to undo the four self-tapping screws which hold the heater outlet seal plate (with the demister elbows sticking out) onto the bulkhead, slacken one of the hose clamps, remove that hose and pull the assembly out of the way.

The heater cab/screen control cable is affixed to the bottom of the heater unit by two bolts which can be seen through the outlet plate aperture (use a torch) when the heater assembly is raised slightly (you'll probably have to break the seal to get it to move). The $5/16$" headed bolt on the cable outer clamp can just be reached though the aperture. To slacken the $1/4$" head bolt which holds the cable inner, use a socket with a 10" extension bar, offered through the driver's side footwell air outlet. Pull the cable away. The heater unit may now be lifted out. When you come to re-fit the heater unit, it is suggested that you connect the cable firstly and feed the end of this through the grommet into the car before lowering the heater into position – it's a real pain trying to fit the cable end once the heater is in situ.

Fitting the improved matrix is simplicity

itself. The heater unit is held together by external spring clips; remove these and you're faced with a simple swap. Do take the opportunity to check that the control flap in the base of the heater unit moves freely, and treat it to a little lithium grease before re-fitting.

ELECTRICS

It is imperative that modifications to the electrical circuits of a car are carried out only by qualified auto-electricians.

WINDSCREEN WASHERS

Early MGBs are fitted with a manual pump which, in its twilight years, can prove rather less than adequate – the pump on the author's '66 GT used to need no less than sixty pumps to prime it and after this effort he was rewarded with no more than a trickle of water on the screen.

This created extra fun at MOT time, because the tester flatly refused to sit there and give the pump the full sixty strokes. The solution chosen by the author was to fit an electric pump/bottle – in fact, one which had been kindly donated by a neighbour (for use on a fishing boat wheelhouse screen) and which was originally sold for use on the rear window of a van or hatchback. This comprises a bottle with an integral pump, so that the electrics are isolated completely from the bodyshell, allowing the unit to be used on an early positive-earth car (provided that the live terminal is fully insulated). The output hose from the unit can be connected to the existing pump/bottle hose end, so that it feeds though the old pump bulb (and can be used to prime it) or it can be connected to the old pump outlet hose to feed the washers direct.

These bottle/pump units are widely available at motor accessory shops, although if your car has a negative earth (Mk.2 onwards), you could fit an electric pump from almost any scrap car

It is a bit awkward to check the battery when it is in position, but take the opportunity to check the charging rate by checking the voltage with the engine running, both with all electrical devices switched off and on. See Chapter four for more details.

into the 'B; all that is necessary is to screw the pump onto the bulkhead near the washer bottle, to cut the existing bottle outlet hose and place each cut end onto the pump inlet and outlet.

In either case, it is recommended that an in-line fuse is fitted to the power supply and, rather than drilling a hole in the dashboard to mount the operating switch, it is recommended that the switch is housed in a separate bracket. If you are unsure of where to take the electric feed for the pump from (and this can vary with the year of the car) then consult an auto-electrician – DON'T just hook up to the nearest live circuit – you might overload it.

Alternatively, replacement pump units are widely available and relatively easy to fit. The author has now, partly as a gesture towards authenticity, removed the electric pump and replaced the old manual pump with a functional one taken from a 1974 Midget – it's exactly the same unit.

If your manual pump always needs a lot of strokes just to prime it, renew the pick-up valve in the reservoir and, if the problem persists, fit a line valve between the pump and jets.

SPOT AND FOG LIGHTS

The most useful of these extra lights is the rear fog light which, on a foggy high speed road can save lives – including yours!

Spotlights pose their own problems. It appears that many countries have their own sets of laws governing the intensity and placement of all extra car lighting. These restrictions are usually given as a maximum wattage of the lights and a minimum/maximum above-road height and distancing in the case of twin spotlights. Those with rubber bumper cars may find it very difficult to comply with local legislation in this respect, and those with chrome bumpered cars may find that the necessary placement of spotlights restricts the flow of air through the radiator intake grille – not a good idea.

Whether or not to fit spotlights is therefore by no means an easy decision. The standard headlights of even the early MGB have in the opinion of the author been quite adequate for all but competitive rally driving, and so the gain brought by spotlights is really very small. Against this, the drawbacks also include high battery drain, which can be a problem on cars

Brown wire solenoid. On early cars, the thick brown wire on the starter solenoid feeds all circuits – disconnecting it knocks out all the electrics apart from the main starter wiring, so if you think you detect a whiff of smoke in the car, pull the brown wire off as soon as possible to prevent a fire.

fitted with the earlier dynamo. If you do wish to fit spotlights then you are advised to first ascertain whether it will be possible to place them in such a position on your car so as to comply with local legislation, and never situate them in front of the radiator grille, because if you do then you'll rob the oil cooler radiator, engine coolant radiator and the engine bay itself from some of its free flow of cooling air. It is also advised that the spotlights have their own fused circuit independent of the rest of the lights.

Again, it is as well to consult an auto-electrician before fitting spot lights, not only to find the best electrical feed but also to gauge the drain which lights of various wattage will place on the battery and generator. Two 55 watt lamps, for instance, will draw 9 amps (wattage = voltage x current) and can on their own fully discharge a 60 amp hour battery in just over six hours. If you want to get serious, add up the current demands of all devices which might be simultaneously switched on in the worst scenario – spotlights, headlights, tail lights, ignition, windscreen wipers, rear screen demister on GTs and also the heater on a cold, rainy night – and compare this with the output of

your generator. If the demands can exceed the supply, then you will be draining the battery – not a good idea.

If you possess a good automotive multimeter, connect this across the battery terminals with the engine running and the scale set to voltage to read in the range of twelve to perhaps fifteen or more volts. Switch everything on, and see how well your generator is charging the battery – anything less than 13 volts indicates that the battery is being drained (over 14.5 volts is over-charging, indicating control box – dynamo – or alternator problems which, if left to their own devices, will boil the electrolyte and ruin the battery).

Sadly, multiple pile-ups on motorways are a feature of modern driving life and better rear illumination might help to cut the number of instances. A fog light should ideally possess its own fused circuit, and the switch should be positioned so that it cannot be inadvertently operated.

Spot lamps have a high current requirement, and if you were to merely hook them up to the headlight feed then you run a real risk of overloading this. The smart way is to use the existing feed from the lighting switch to power a separate relay, to wire the relay directly to the battery main feed and to power the spot lamps from this. This way, the spot lamps can only operate when the headlamps are on, but the relay power requirement from the headlamp circuit is minuscule.

With the fitting of lights, incidentally, owners of early positive earth cars do not have to worry about polarity – lights work whichever way the current passes through them!

Chapter six contains an introduction to electricity, and reading this will give a fuller understanding of the subject.

BATTERY ISOLATOR

Electrical fires in old cars occur frequently enough to be a serious worry, and can reduce a car to a burnt-out shell in a matter of minutes if the fire originates close to inflammable brake/clutch fluid, petrol or upholstery. The author has first-hand experience of an electrical fire: it occurred behind the dashboard of his '66 GT while the car was parked on his drive. It was no more than perhaps twenty or thirty seconds before the interior of the car was filled with choking fumes and, by the time luggage from the rear seat, the seat base and the battery cover had been thrown out onto the lawn so that the battery earth terminal could be disconnected, the permanently live (brown) wires concerned had burnt away the majority of their insulation.

With the panic over, it was immediately obvious that, instead of disconnecting the battery, all the author had needed to do was to pull the thick brown feed wire which runs from the starter solenoid to the regulator (cars fitted with a dynamo only), because the current for all electrical devices on early cars is fed through this wire. The cause of the fire turned out to be an un-insulated spade connector (fitted by a previous owner) dropping off its terminal on the radio and shorting to earth. It nearly cost the author his beloved car.

Electrical fires start because current passes through a wire at a higher amperage (current) than the wire is able to tolerate – usually when un-insulated wire, terminals or part of an electrical component touches earth (the bodywork of the car) – without a load in the (shortened) circuit, the battery discharges at its maximum rate and the wire concerned becomes hot then melts its insulation which eventually catches fire. Most circuits are fused – that is, they contain a special length of wire which has no insulation and which is designed to burn through safely if the current which passes through it is higher than a pre-determined level. Not all circuits, however, contain fuses. The lighting and ignition circuits usually have none.

There is a strong case for fitting a battery isolation switch which, when operated, disconnects the earth terminal from the bodywork, so preventing current from flowing in any wires. The type of switch the MGB owner needs is that found on competition cars rather than types which fit to the battery earth post itself (the battery being situated under a cover plate which takes time to remove); these can be obtained from most motor accessory shops. To fit them, the author would suggest drilling a mounting hole through the heelboard.

Again, an auto-electrician will undertake the fitting of this switch and, unless you know what you are doing, it is recommended that you take this option.

AMMETER/VOLTMETER

An ammeter measures current flow and can be used to check whether the battery is being charged or discharged. Unfortunately, the ammeter has to be wired so that it measures all current flow except that which operates the starter motor. In order to wire an ammeter you have to run very thick wire behind the dashboard, with obvious safety hazards. A voltmeter

– sometimes referred to as a 'battery condition meter' – is a far more sensible option which shows the state of the battery (ignition 'on' but engine not running) and the charge rates.

IN-CAR ENTERTAINMENT

In-car entertainment (ICE) equipment is a catch-all term nowadays applied to radios, cassette players, graphic equalisers and compact disc players.

Those with early cars might like to try and fit a basic period radio unit which is in keeping with the general character of their car. These units can be obtained from some specialists who have (showing great foresight) rescued many such radios over the years from scrapped cars, then serviced them and placed them into storage for future sale. These radios will not be cheap and you may in fact be asked to pay more than the price of a far better modern alternative.

Modern ICE equipment is often very different from the equivalent which might have typically been fitted to a new MGB. Not only has the range of types of equipment grown, but so have, in some instances, the dimensions. The radio aperture in a pre 1972 chrome bumper MGB dashboard is – at 7" x 2" – simply not large enough to house some of today's more sophisticated ICE equipment, and neither is the subsequent aperture of the centre console on later models. To make matters worse, many people now wish to also fit a graphic equaliser, which no MGB has dedicated space for. In both instances, an alternative site must be sought.

It is possible to hang both the central ICE unit plus a graphic equaliser underneath the dashboard of the car, using the standard Meccano-like strips of metal which are provided for the purpose with most of this equipment. The drawbacks to doing this are that there is not too much depth between the floor and dashboard of the MGB and so passenger's legs may foul deeper ICE units as they climb into or out of the seat. Another problem is theft.

Theft of modern ICE equipment from parked cars is rife and the ragtop of the MGB roadster means that a thief need not even possess the skill needed to break into a car in order to steal ICE equipment from a roadster – he can simply slash the hood open. If you are in two minds whether to fit a basic unit into the proper aperture or an expensive unit slung under the dash, bear in mind that thieves tend to steal only the better quality ICE equipment!

GENERAL INSTALLATION NOTES

Other electrical equipment in the car can cause interference and unwanted speaker noise when the car radio is in use. In general, you should try to keep components and leads – including the aerial lead – as far away from all elements of the ignition and direction indicator circuits as possible. Check that the unit has a good earth and the correct 1 amp or 2 amp in-line fuse fitted. Also fit an in-line choke (available – as are other electrical components mentioned here – at motor factors or radio shops) in the electrical supply to the radio, preferably as close as possible to the unit.

Using carbon rather than copper cored high tension leads removes one potential source of interference and is a more elegant solution than using resistive plug caps or in-line resistors in the HT leads.

The generator and contact breaker point ignition have the potential to cause interference; fit a .1 mf capacitor between an earth and the coil positive terminal, and another in between earth and the large terminal on the generator. Electronic ignition systems have built-in suppression – don't fit a capacitor to the coil in this instance because you risk damaging the system if you do.

If, after taking the steps outlined here, interference is still a problem then there are specialist works available which may be able to help; alternatively, consult a specialist.

EARLY CARS

Fitting modern electronic equipment in a Mk.1 MGB poses special problems due to the car's positive earth electrics. If you were to pump electricity through the integrated circuits backwards then you would instantly ruin the equipment concerned! There are three alternative methods of fitting such equipment. The easiest is to obtain a modern radio which works with a positive earthed car, and these (including stereo radio/cassette players) are available from a few companies which advertise in the classic car press, or to seek out a reconditioned period radio. The second method – which is NOT recommended – is to completely isolate the metal chassis of the radio from the metal of the car body, but this is not too easy a solution and is not recommended because it makes the radio chassis 'live'; that is, if any metal part of the car comes into contact with it then a short circuit and a blown fuse – or possibly an electrical fire – will result.

The most drastic but often the favoured solution to the problem of a positive earthed car is to reverse the polarity. This is not too difficult a task, because most of the car instruments and standard electrical components will work without problem.

Remove the twin (standard) or single (modification) batteries, and take the opportunity to clean them and to clean the terminal posts. Replace the earth strap with one which has the correct sized clamp for the negative battery post. Gently apply heat to the old wiring terminal caps or clamps (the caps were original equipment; on many cars they will have been replaced with clamps) until they can be pulled off, and either swap the positive and negative caps or preferably fit modern clamps. Before reconnecting the batteries (you will have to fit them the other way around, of course), ensure that the ignition switch is turned off.

Swap the white and white/black wires on the coil (the white must go to the positive terminal

and vice versa). Remove the brown/green wire from the field (F) terminal of the dynamo and, using a length of wire, make a momentary connection between the field terminal and a live terminal (use the starter solenoid post). This reverses the polarity of the dynamo. Replace the brown/green wire. Run the engine for a few seconds, but be ready to immediately turn the ignition off (or have an assistant ready to) and pull the brown wire from the starter solenoid if the ignition warning light fails to go out when the ignition is turned off. If this happens, methodically check your work and re-polarise the dynamo.

The last task is to remove the tachometer from the dashboard (it is held by knurled wheel nuts behind the dashboard) and to cut, swap and re-join the two sections of the white wire which is looped at the rear of the unit (cut through the wires and fit barrel-type connectors to re-join them or preferably use solder and heat-shrink insulation).

Carefully remove the bezel and glass from the front of the unit, undo the two screws at the rear which hold the internals in position and slide the mechanism out from the casing. Reverse the polarity of the live and earth wires. Unsolder the end of the resistor which is attached to the spade terminal and re-attach it to the post to the left of the spade terminal. This work is probably best undertaken by an auto-electrician or, alternatively, acquire a negative earth tachometer and fit that!

FIRE EXTINGUISHER

A small automotive 1kg or 2kg dry power fire extinguisher can be mounted fairly inconspicuously on the heelboard of both roadsters and GTs or, alternatively, on the passenger side footwell. These units can, however, give greatly differing performances – some are not very good whilst other, almost identical, units can be very efficient. Consult any major motoring organisation to which you belong for a recommendation – that's what they're there for! At a higher price, under bonnet fixed extinguishers are available; some are operated manually from within the cab and others are automatic. To rely on one of these units alone is questionable, because fires don't start only under the bonnet. If you can afford one great, but still fit a small extinguisher inside the cab.

HANDLING MODIFICATIONS

The MGB was never intended to be an out and out performance car. It was designed to be a comfortable long distance sports tourer, and its suspension is consequently quite soft and has a fair range of travel. Some owners like to stiffen the suspension up.

Before considering any modifications, do reflect that the pre-1974 chrome bumper MGB and MGB GT actually handle quite well, hold the road reasonably for cars of their vintage and are safe and very predictable at all normal road speeds – a real pleasure to drive. The black bumper cars are less good in both roadholding and handling, and it is suggested that owners of these later cars simply lower the ride height (several companies sell excellent kits for the purpose) which, in itself, will give such a vast improvement in road manners that further work will usually be deemed unnecessary.

Roadholding is simply a measure of the traction of the tyres under a variety of conditions, handling is the poise of the car when undergoing manoeuvres; the two are interrelated but individual. A car with good roadholding but not such good handling can be driven very hard but will make great demands upon the skills and efforts of the driver; a car with less impressive roadholding but good handling can be driven at slightly lesser speeds but with little effort on the part of the driver. Remember that play or wear in some of the suspension/steering components can have a marked effect on both handling and roadholding. Before consid-

ering any modification of your car's suspension, therefore, do check that the dampers and springs are in good condition, that the wishbone bushes on the front suspension are not perished, that the kingpins don't have play and that the steering rack and the steering column universal joint have no play in them.

Another point to consider before attacking the suspension is the fact that most modifications will have a small but noticeable effect on ride comfort. The majority of modifications therefore to some degree trade off better roadholding or handling against the comfort levels experienced by the driver and passengers.

Don't place too much importance on how competition cars are set up, because some of the modifications which are widely carried out on the suspensions of competition cars are far too extreme for any road-going car.

The MGB in all its guises is prone to (arguably excessive) body roll on hard cornering (a handling characteristic). Whilst this is not necessarily a bad thing, a rapid shift of direction followed by a correction (for instance, swerving to avoid some obstacle in the road and pulling back in before the suspension has had time to re-settle) can make the suspension on each side of the car move from one extreme to the other – from tension to compression and vice-versa – reducing tyre grip: and many people like to reduce the amount by which the body is able to roll. This can be achieved in a variety of ways. The most obvious is to fit anti-roll bars or uprated anti-roll bars in the case of cars which already have standard bars.

An anti roll bar is a 'U' shaped torsion spring which connects the suspension either side of the car. If one side is compressed, this places a force on the anti-roll bar which, in turn places a lesser force on the other side of the suspension. The result is that the car remains flatter on corners. Don't be tempted to obtain and fit anti-roll bars other than in sets which have been specially designed for the MGB, such as the Ron Hopkinson Handling kit. These have been designed to work with the standard MGB springing and damping; fitting odd anti-roll bars could make the combined handling and road grip of the car dangerous.

Alternatively, you could opt to stiffen up the suspension generally by fitting sturdier springs and dampers. Again, you should choose one of the widely available and competition-proven kits rather than cobbling something together yourself. Springs and dampers have to be matched; too strong a spring for the damper will result in reduced road-holding and too strong a damper for the spring will prevent the spring from absorbing shocks from the tyres effectively, and transmit huge stresses to the damper mounting points, giving a very harsh ride. Still with the subject of handling kits, the MG Owners' Club offers two; the first is an uprated front anti-roll bar which lessens the body roll potential at the front of the car and so reduces understeer; kit two includes this and two 'A' frames which help rear axle location and also cut down on wheel tramp. The 'A' frames are available separately, and should give worthwhile improvements if used in conjunction with other modifications.

The various kits are usually compatible; but before bolting various handling goodies to your car, do check with all of the suppliers concerned that they are compatible with any other components which you have fitted or intend to fit. Most suppliers are fully familiar with their competitor's uprated suspension components or kits, and will be able to advise on worthwhile combinations.

One deservedly popular modification is to fit modern telescopic dampers, which are also widely available, complete with fitting kits designed specifically for the MGB. Because the original front dampers form the top link of the suspension, some people who have fitted telescopic dampers have been faced with MOT failures in the UK when fluid has been discovered on the old (unused) damper body: if this happens, contact the nearest Ministry of

Transport testing centre, and they will deal with the testing station on your behalf.

The fitting of wider wheels (which must be guarded by wider wheel arches in the UK) is not generally recommended for normal road use. Firstly, wider wheels place greater strain on the wheel bearings, as do, incidentally, spacers which increase the track; secondly, they add to the general softness of the suspension. Furthermore, having wider wheels and tyres won't necessarily place more rubber in contact with the road. The tyre contact area can be calculated by dividing the weight of the vehicle by the tyre pressure in pounds per square inch (psi). In round figures, a car weighing 2,000 lbs with tyre pressures of 25 psi will have a total tyre contact area (a 'footprint') of 2000/25 or 80 square inches – 20 square inches per tyre – irrespective of the width of the tyre. There are positive drawbacks to the fitting of wider tyres, including higher replacement costs, greater rolling and air resistance. By fitting wide wheels you are also unwittingly throwing out a challenge to every boy racer in a 'hot hatch' who sees you on the road...

Low profile tyres have in recent years become very popular, both as original equipment and after-market add-ons. These tyres are not as good at absorbing shocks as normal profile tyres, and their use is questionable on those MGBs to which they can be fitted.

SECURITY DEVICES

An MGB – any MGB (including the GT, C and V8, chrome or black bumper) – is a valuable motor car. Even restoration project B's are worth money as donors for re-shelling projects. Little wonder that MGBs get stolen.

The modern solution to automotive theft is to fit ever-more sophisticated electronic alarm systems but, as the systems become more complex, so new means are devised by criminals to overcome them. At the time of writing, so-called 'grabber' devices are widely available, able to de-cipher the electronic codes used on the most sophisticated alarm systems. If you wish to have an alarm in your car then take advice from your local Crime Prevention Officer and have the device fitted by professionals.

Alternative physical anti-theft devices fare little better. Steering locks can be broken, as can many of the third-party devices which clamp on to the steering wheel, pedals, handbrake lever or a combination of these. If an accomplished and determined thief wants your car then he or she will usually succeed.

Firstly, there are security measures which you can take whenever you have to leave your car locked in your garage or parked on your driveway for any period of time – say, more than a few days. Disconnecting the battery and removing the earth strap (or even the battery) takes maybe ten minutes, removing the distributor cap and/or rotor arm takes even less time – both will stop most thieves, because few will be armed with the components which you have removed to disable the car.

If your car is to be laid up over the winter months as many MGBs are, then you can go further; why not raise the car and support it on axle stands, remove the road wheels and store these away separately. Removing the steering wheel necessitates undoing just one large nut and, coupled with the other suggestions above, can prove to be the last straw as far as a would-be thief is concerned.

So-called 'joyriders' who steal cars in order to drive them at breakneck speeds present another problem for the MGB owner. Although these people generally prefer the hot hatch type of car, an MGB will undoubtedly appeal to many. Joyriders don't steal the car for financial gain, and hence they are have no compunction in doing whatever damage proves necessary to get the engine going and the car on the move. Physical locking devices will dissuade many from attempting to take a car, but some of these devices are sadly liable to be

kicked or hammered off, so choose carefully.

The best way to prevent theft, in the opinion of the author, is to dissuade the thief from stealing the car rather than trying to prevent him from doing so. The motive for most thefts being the financial profit from the subsequent sale of the vehicle, you can dissuade the thief by marking the car's registration number onto as many components as possible. This is just an extension of having the registration number engraved onto the windows, but very effective, because at a stroke, you prevent the thief from giving the car a false set of plates and selling it, and also from breaking the car for spares.

Security marking kits, containing stencils and engraving, indelible ink and other markers, are widely available and, armed with such a kit, there are few components which cannot be marked with the car's registration number.

UNDER THE BONNET

Many people replace the mechanically driven radiator cooling fan with an electric alternative, which should give a small gain in general fuel efficiency both by allowing the engine to come to operating temperature more rapidly and by removing the need for the engine to physically drive the fan. Apart from the fitting of the fan (which comes with full instructions), all you have to do is de-tension the fan belt, unbolt the existing fan, then replace the water pump pulley using new lock washers and re-tension the belt.

Breakerless ignition (usually referred to as electronic ignition) replaces the contact breaker points and condenser with a unit which employs an electronic or photo-electronic sensor and pole piece to control the coil discharge. This cuts maintenance time slightly and – more importantly – should prove more reliable than a points and condenser system.

Breakerless conversion kits are also available for SU fuel pumps; these replace the contact breaker points with an electronic alternative, and so again make the car more reliable.

CHAPTER THREE

Surviving Restorers and Restoration

Before embarking on a DIY restoration or commissioning a professional restoration, do take time to consider whether it might be better to simply buy a ready-restored car. Few professionally or even DIY restored cars are worth anywhere near their combined purchase and restoration costs and, by buying a ready restored car, you will be benefiting from the loss which the unfortunate vendor will inevitably have to take on the deal.

Many dreams have turned into nightmares when MGBs have been restored, both by professional restoration companies and by DIY-inclined owners. The most frequent and most obvious danger area is finance – when the cash runs out before the car is finished – but there are a host of other pitfalls which call for real survival expertise. It can cost more to restore a poor MGB body than it would cost to buy a brand-new Heritage bodyshell. Heritage shells are electrophoretically primed, should outlast restored shells and are highly recommended for both DIY and professional restorations. Bodywork repair is, however, only part of the story

Few people appreciate just how great an undertaking a complete classic car restoration is. Most published works on the subject deal with specific areas which require expertise and knowledge such as welding, mechanical repair and paint spraying, but fail to inform the reader that these tasks represent but a fraction of the work which goes into a restoration. Painting a car, for instance, takes only minutes in terms of the actual spraying: in order that those few minutes' work should give good results it is necessary to spend weeks – sometimes months if you are working on a part-time basis – in preparation.

Don't be fooled into thinking that a part-restoration is any easier. You might set out, for instance, to re-spray just the engine bay. However, as you remove components from the bay you will discover that many need replacement or at the very least cleaning and re-painting. The very act of removing some components might damage them or more usually their seized fittings and necessitate their repair or replacement. As you strip paint you will usually find areas of rot which have to be cut out and have new steel welded in. Then there's the problem of knowing where to stop, because a shiny engine bay really cries out for a shiny engine, radiator and so on. You'll probably then wish to spray the bonnet and wings so that their condition and colour matches that of the engine bay, then the doors, then the rear wings, and so on.

Every part of the car which you work on will serve only to show up other areas which require attention because they look shabby in comparison. Most part-restorations grow into full restorations. Most DIY full restorations take years.

Restoration is not a cheap way to acquire a good car. It is not a way to make money. In short, embark on a restoration only if the process of restoration rather than ownership of the finished car is the end.

SURVIVING RESTORERS

There are many good and trustworthy individuals and businesses in the fields of automotive mechanical repair and in restoration. There are also scoundrels. To the 'man in the street', the entire automotive trade can be a jungle in which survival can be a matter of luck – he can be fortunate and deal with an honest and scrupulous business, or unlucky and in his innocence deal with a rogue. Without knowledge of the 'black arts' of the mechanic, he can get ripped off by a rascal even during a simple service through work being charged for but not done, components listed on the bill but not fitted. With restoration the stakes – and with them the risks – rise.

While it is generally true that a little learning is a dangerous thing, having some understanding of what maintenance and repair work entails can be the very best safeguard against being cheated if you have your car maintained or repaired professionally. Similarly, the key to surviving professional restorers is knowing a lot about the subject of restoration, even if you don't possess the actual skills to carry out a restoration or even to place a bead of weld yourself. In other words, you need to become an 'armchair expert' by reading as much as possible about the subject.

Before you first make contact with a restorer you should then be able to carry out a fairly comprehensive pre-restoration inspection yourself and draw up a list of jobs which need to be done. Don't show your list to the restorer, but keep it to compare with the work listed on the estimate when it arrives following the restorer's appraisal of your car. If you go to an out and out rogue without this knowledge, you are at his mercy and the estimate could contain much work which is unnecessary, and some (for which you will be charged) which is not necessary and, in the event, might not actually be carried out. You might find that there is no mention of a body panel which you know to be in need of replacement – for instance, a castle rail – which tells you that it is the restorer's intention to patch repair this – unacceptable practice. Worse, you could be on the receiving end of a telephone call – part-way through the restoration when the car cannot be moved without causing terminal distortion of the bodyshell – to inform you that a need for further essential, and very expensive repair work has come to light.

Step One in finding a good restorer is to talk to satisfied and dissatisfied owners of restored MGBs; you can find plenty of these at your local MG club branch, and even more at any of the major MGB or general classic car shows. The beauty of consulting local people is that they will be able to recommend (or warn you off) local restoration companies. But don't take their word for it; examine their cars in minute detail, looking for rippling of body panels (shoddy finishing of areas covered with body filler or distortion during welding), door fit and, if the owners will permit, lift the door surround trim, count the thicknesses of steel at the sill top and the welding method used to join them – if there are other than three thicknesses then the extras are the remains of rotted former sill panels which, in the worst cases, could simply have been hammered inwards to be covered by a new outer sill (which will rot very quickly). If the sill top seam is gas welded then the restorer is not so well equipped as to possess a spot welder, a negative point. Use a magnet to reveal any holes bridged with GRP or really deep dents full of bodyfiller. Check that the condition of the visible part of the outer sill is not better than that of the quarter panel right behind it – if it is better then you are looking at centre sill cover panels.

Don't be guided purely by how smart a car looks. The author has known of some really eye-catching 'restored' MGBs which were in fact very good bodges and which, within three to at most five years, usually either have to be re-bodged (more patches welded on) or restored properly when they fail the MOT due to bodywork weaknesses. A full guide to appraising MGBs is given in the book *MGB Restoration/Preparation/Maintenance* published by Osprey.

Step Two is to arrange to visit restorers who make it onto your short list. Turn up a little earlier than expected so that you see the workshop in its usual state rather than after it has been tidied up to put on a good show to impress you – which does happen. Appearances are important. A good restoration workshop will have the following. MGBs undergoing restoration. An MGB-owning boss and preferably MGB-owning staff. Plenty of room and light, and a water-tight roof. Good quality tools neatly and methodically stored away so that they can quickly be found when needed. Spot, MiG and gas welding equipment. A pit or preferably a car lift. Staff who don't smoke in the workshop and who use appropriate safety equipment, such as gauntlets and eye protection. Combustible materials stored safely away in an outside building. The very best businesses will also have a spares sales division, and hence a good range of spares on site, and all bought in at trade prices.

A bad restoration workshop will possess the following. A wide variety of cars in various states of decay or part-restored in and around the workshop. Cramped working conditions, poor lighting and a leaking roof. Poor quality tools strewn about the floor so that the staff waste hours looking for the right tool. Only gas welding equipment. Surly or over-frivolous staff whose cigarette ends lie where they fall on the floor. Tins of thinners stored next to gas heaters.

All restorers nowadays should possess either MiG or Tig welding equipment. If you see only gas welding gear then this is not a good sign. Painting should not be undertaken in a general body shop, because the air will inevitably be full of particles of dust, silicones and other contaminants which make it difficult if not impossible to achieve good results. If a separate paint booth is not to be seen on site, the better restorer will sub-contract this part of the restoration to someone with the proper facilities.

Examine work in progress. Your knowledge of restoration – gleaned from reading books and articles on the subject – should enable you to assess good and bad practices. For instance, observe whether all rot is cut out or whether new panels are welded on top of hammered-in existing ones (common and very poor practice). Note how bodyshells are supported for major welded repairs – it being all too easy to distort especially the Roadster shell through poor support when the sills have been cut away. Check that reasonable rust-resisting measures are taken such as coating seams which are to be welded with zinc paint and using seam sealer on them afterwards. A few unscrupulous individuals have been known to deliberately ignore rust-retarding techniques and practices, because this helps generate future bodywork repair business for them – be warned.

Most professional restorers nowadays use body filler in moderation and, in fact, there is nothing at all wrong with this because, correctly used on clean and rust-free steel in no more than a thin skim, bodyfiller will probably outlast the panels to which it is applied. If you see a five litre tin of the stuff in the premises of a restorer who only works on one car at a time, however, then it is difficult not to conclude that he uses huge dollops of filler to mask shoddy workmanship. GRP repair materials are another matter; these are used to bridge holes which should ideally be welded (whereas body filler should only be used to build up the surface in shallow dents). If you see GRP repair kits or materials lying around (and unless the business restores GRP bodied cars like the Scimitar and TVRs) walk away.

Attitudes are equally important. The boss should not try too hard to appear to be your pal or hint at 'special deals' involving VAT-free cash payment and the like, should not be brusque, but simply businesslike and give the impression of efficiency. The staff should be friendly enough to exchange pleasantries with you but not so chatty that they are distracted from their work by engaging you in long conversations – the owner of the car currently being restored will in effect be paying for the staff to thus entertain you, and you will similarly have to pay them to chat to other droppers-in if they restore your car. Generally, you should trust your instincts and, if you feel uncomfortable in any way with the business, the staff or the premises then it's best to look elsewhere.

Ask whether you will be welcome to call in occasionally during the restoration – if not, it's because there is likely to be something in the workshop that is not for your eyes, such as the Boss' car being serviced in workshop time you are paying for, or a rusted panel on your car being hammered inwards before a cover plate is welded on top.

Insist on a full photographic record being kept of the restoration. This not only proves to you that the work you are being charged for gets done, it is a record of the work which you can show to any potential buyer in the future if, for some unfathomable reason, you should ever decide to sell your MGB. If a restorer refuses this request or tries to put you off the idea by telling you that it will add inordinately to the bill, walk away, because the restorer has something to hide. Ask to see photographs of previous restorations, too. In these days of cheap colour processing, there is no excuse for any restorer not to keep photographic records of his work.

Next comes the problem of assessing the various estimates given for the work. Very high or very low estimates should be treated with caution – go for one near the average. The estimate should list all necessary work, all components and materials, and show labour charges and hours.

A competent and well-run business will furnish a comprehensive estimate; if all you get is a vague set of figures scribbled on a scrap of paper then expect standards of workmanship to be similarly lax. It is best to obtain three or more estimates if possible.

There are basically two types of restoration company. Some have superbly equipped workshops and hourly labour charges which reflect their high overheads; others might operate out of low-cost premises and lack expensive equip-

ment, and should consequently have much lower hourly labour charges. The latter type of business might at first sight appear to be the cheaper option, but the better equipped business should be able to complete the work in a much shorter time, so that the total labour charge can be lower. In either case, always remember that a restoration company which specialises in MGBs will take less time to complete the work than a non-specialist – however good they are.

It is always a good idea to show estimates to fellow enthusiasts, who might spot some discrepancy which has evaded your attention, or perhaps be able to 'read between the lines' and discover evidence of poor working practice. For instance, the knowledgeable enthusiast might note that a lower front wing repair panel is listed on the estimate (possibly only as a catalogue code number), which means that the restorer intends to cut the bottom off what might be a perfectly sound front wing in order to avoid the time-consuming business of removing it. This practice is widespread, but not good because it means that the car will have one extra welded seam per side, and repair work usually rusts out first along welded seams.

Remember that there are numerous permutations of price and job specifications; these can usually be juggled to a compromise which suits your own pocket and aspirations. You might, for instance, elect to remove the front wings yourself and save several hours' labour charges; if the estimate is 'modular' – each component of the job is costed separately – then you can select which jobs you feel confident you can do yourself, and which you would rather entrust to the professional.

Expect to have to pay a deposit on commissioning the work, and in some cases 'stage' payments as the job progresses. These payments should not come to more than the components and consumables which have to be bought in at the time the payment becomes due.

The result of several months of hard labour. Is it worth it? Of course it is. Having a smart engine bay means that, unlike so many MGB owners, you are not afraid to open your car's bonnet in polite company.

Ensure that your car will be fully insured against accidental damage while on the restorer's premises, and also that you have cover should the car be stolen or returned to you in an unacceptable or unsafe state. Use an insurance broker who specialises in the classic car market, and check the terms and conditions of your policy before taking the car to your chosen restorer. The restorer should also be insured, and if he cannot show you proof of insurance cover then go elsewhere.

It is, of course, during the restoration that relations between you and the restorer can become most strained. There exists a fine line which separates keeping a watchful eye on the restoration and being a pain in the butt, and another which separates keeping the Boss on his or her toes and annoying them sufficiently to incite them to do something nasty to your car – cross them at your peril.

Disputes between you and the restorer should be settled easily, amicably and quickly; if a dispute cannot be settled during a friendly discussion, you're in trouble. You have all the power of modern consumer law on your side; the restorer has your car and a cutting torch, so tread very carefully.

SURVIVING DIY RESTORATION

Few first-time restorers realise just how much work goes into a restoration; some take months, some years and a large percentage are never finished at all. A lot of heartache could be avoided by starting off with a realistic appraisal of the facilities at your disposal, your skills and most especially your dogged determination to see the job through.

How well do you cope with setbacks? If you are the kind of person who is likely to go into deep depression when the paint topcoat blisters or the clutch master cylinder leaks fluid onto your shiny new paintwork, then perhaps you are not really suited to restoration.

Then consider the financial aspect of the restoration. Carry out an appraisal of the car; bodywork, mechanical components and trim. Cost the exercise out, not forgetting to account for paint, welding consumables and so on. Look at the total projected cost and consider whether it might be better to sell your own car and buy a ready-restored one instead. It usually is.

Few first-time restorers appreciate just how

expensive a DIY restoration can be; in 1994 at the time of writing it is easy to approach or even exceed five-figure sums on MGB repair panels (or a new bodyshell), plus mechanical and electrical components during a restoration. If you wish to rebuild a car to as-new condition then unfortunately you're going to have to pay out as much as you would have to in order to buy a new car – and not an economy saloon car, but a modern sports car. The only way to bring costs substantially down is to clean and re-use tired components instead of acquiring exchange reconditioned or newly-manufactured ones. This is fine for a car which is to receive light and occasional use, but for a car which is to be relied upon for daily transport it is folly.

This brings us to the question of where to obtain spares. The author has found that some MGB specialists are better than others in that some are staffed by very knowledgeable MGB enthusiasts whilst others have staff whose lack of specialised knowledge can result in your being sold the 'wrong' spare for the year of your MGB. The better spares suppliers all tend to incorporate workshop and sometimes full restoration facilities, so that the staff all acquire an excellent all-round working knowledge.

Even so, one of the very best investments the MGB owner can make is a manufacturer's parts catalogue, which gives the correct code number for each and every spare. Armed with this, there should be no room for misunderstanding.

RESTORATION vs RECONSTRUCTION

There is an important distinction to be made between restoration and reconstructing. Restoration pure might be better termed 'renovation', because it involves stripping components, repairing, rebuilding and repainting them, whereas we fortunate MGB owners who have easy access to new and reconditioned spares can take the easier (but more expensive) route of simply acquiring new or exchange reconditioned components – everything from a bolt to a bodyshell. This latter course is actually reconstruction rather than restoration, and the greater the emphasis on reconstruction in a restoration the higher the eventual cost.

Of course, the great overhead in renovation is the time requirement, and the trade-off is thus our time and effort versus our money. Example: your car has a leaking brake calliper, due to a damaged seal. Brakes get very hot, non-silicone brake fluid is combustible, airflow past the calliper will almost certainly blow some fluid onto the disc, reducing braking efficiency. Something, obviously, has to be done. The renovator acquires a seal kit, spends maybe two or three hours repairing the first calliper (this is not an easy repair) and perhaps under an hour on the second – because he now knows exactly what he's doing. The reconstructer unbolts his callipers and exchanges them for reconditioned ones, in the process, spending five to perhaps seven times as much money as the renovator but doing the job in a fraction of the time.

Most MGB restorations appear to be a combination of renovation and reconstruction, with the accent on reconstruction because the MGB is so well served with quality spares. DIY restoration – even in cases where the accent is on renovation – is most certainly not a cheap route to ownership of a nice MGB. In addition to the costs of the actual restoration, most people have to invest quite large sums in the large range of tools which will be needed. Before even that overhead can be taken into consideration, there comes the problem of premises.

PREMISES

MGBs have been restored at the roadside and in polythene-covered lean-tos, but few people will be able to survive such harsh environments for the course of a full restoration (which usually incorporates at least one winter). What you need is a proper workshop.

Wooden buildings have much to commend them – most notably the sound and heat insulation qualities of wood and the fact that the workshop should not suffer from condensation dripping from the roof and down the walls – the greatest drawback of steel buildings; the minus point is the obvious fire hazard. It's bad enough having a car full of inflammable materials and such potentially explosive substances as petrol, thinners and the like in a workshop without also having an inflammable workshop! The alternatives are steel cladding or bricks and mortar. Like the little piggy, build in brick if possible – with steel cladding, condensation in winter can be a real problem and, on hot summer mornings, steel-clad buildings rapidly turn into ovens. As a minimum, the work area should be large enough to accommodate two cars – and preferably three – in order to give sufficient space to restore one.

The tools of restoration are expensive but it is advisable to buy the very best quality you can afford, because cheap tools can fail just as you really need them – and when they break they often damage the components on which they are being used. However, good quality tools are always expensive, and you can, for instance, buy a cheap set of spanners initially, but replace those which wear out (which receive the highest use) with better quality alternatives. You'll probably find that the $7/16$", $1/2$" and $9/16$" spanners succumb to old age first. The same applies to sockets.

Also buy the best in components and consumables. For example, you can find reconditioned exchange gearboxes and engines offered by obscure businesses at very low prices, but it is always better to buy from a recognised specialist supplier and to pay the higher price which they will charge. Cheap paint and thinners will not only jeopardise the paint finish, but will usually be more difficult to work with.

Speaking of paint, most people seem happy to rely on the primer in which repair panels are supplied for rust protection, but since discovering traces of rust under such primer in addition to poor paint adhesion on a batch of cheap wings (*not* MGB), the author now takes all repair panels back to bright metal and primers them himself. Better quality panels will undoubtedly have been properly cleaned before the primer was applied.

Make the workshop more welcoming. Some source of heat in the winter is a must. If there's room, install a chair and a kettle. Get hold of some really nice prints of an MGB which looks just like yours will after the restoration, and plaster the workshop walls with them to help motivate you in moments of gloom. End each session in the workshop by tidying up, so that all of your tools are in their correct places and cleaned of grease ready for the next time.

MENTAL ATTITUDE

In survivalist terms, restoring a car is roughly equivalent to crossing the Atlantic in a bathtub or making it to the South Pole on a pogo stick. I exaggerate, but I'm sure you get the general idea. DIY restoration can be hell.

It's all down to your state of mind. If things are going well then you're bound to be in a good state of mind, but the reason things go well is simply BECAUSE you're in a good state of mind – not the other way around. Consider the opposite scenario; you're feeling depressed, angry or just plain old mentally tired. Your mind is not really on the job and the spanner slips off the nut or the stud shears so that your hand smashes into one of the many and varied sharp objects cunningly placed for this very purpose on the car. State of mind is similarly capable of causing MiG welders to burn through expensive body panels, fresh paint on a perfectly prepared surface to blister and chrome trim to buckle as you're struggling to fit it onto the car.

Few restorations progress without major

setbacks, most normally the discovery of former butchery or bodgery – patches all along the inside of the cross member or rear chassis rails – that sort of thing. Be warned, there can arise situations which can see your mood fluctuating between suicidal and homicidal: I know – I've been there.

What's the remedy? Sniffing thinners generally makes things worse and kicking the car not only makes more work but also hurts your foot. Try walking away from the workshop. Do something completely different; something which you enjoy and which you're good at. Do something which places you in a good frame of mind, and do it for long enough to erase the recent memory of things which went wrong in the restoration.

Of course, prevention is always better than cure, and there are ways in which you can mentally prepare yourself for what could otherwise be fraught sessions in the workshop. Think through the jobs you intend to do, carry them out mentally so that they go without a hitch, and list them so that you don't end up wandering aimlessly around the car wondering what to do next. Install a radio in the workshop and tune in to a station which broadcasts relaxing music rather than frenetic modern stuff or chat shows in which you subconsciously become involved.

Try to become more methodical; keep a list of spares and consumables to be acquired and regularly update this so that you aren't prevented from working for want of a body repair panel or MiG wire. If the job you're doing begins to bore or frustrate you, move on to something else which is more interesting or easier before your mood darkens too much – by the time you return to the original task it will usually progress far more sweetly.

Try to establish a regular working routine; if you are able to spare, say, two hours an evening, then begin work at seven p.m. and leave when the nine o'clock news comes on the radio, because this way, every day you'll see at least some small evidence of progress.

Visitors to your workshop can be a blessing or a bane: only invite fellow DIY (or professional) restorers and keep all sightseers at bay. Lock them out if necessary, because they'll not only distract you with countless pointless questions, the answers to which are of no benefit to them and are instantly forgotten, but they are likely to lean on freshly painted bodywork, tread on repair panels and kick over tins of paint.

A visit from a fellow restorer, on the other hand, is most likely to inject new enthusiasm into the project as the visitor rolls his or (occasionally) her sleeves up and gets stuck in. It's always more fun working on someone else's car and, when you suddenly find an enthusiastic volunteer helping in the Good Work, you'll want to work as well.

Never be afraid to call in professional assistance. It would, for instance, work out cheaper to have sills welded up professionally than to attempt the work yourself and have to replace the lot if your welding proves less than perfect! Similarly, it can prove less expensive to have the paint preparation and spraying carried out professionally than to have to buy a decent compressor, oil/water filter and spraygun, not to mention two or more lots of paint if things go wrong – and be warned that things often go wrong when amateurs point a spray gun at a car!

Although many of the people who claim to have fully restored their cars have actually brought in professionals to do much (in many cases, most) of the work and are happy to bask in the reflected glory of the professional's work, there is no shame in admitting such involvement and certainly no glory in attempting tasks beyond your abilities and making a mess of things. Your life could depend on the quality of the welding, in the integrity of the wiring, the efficiency of the braking system – once the car is out on the roads. Don't risk it – summon professional help whenever you feel the slightest bit out of your depth.

STRIPDOWN

Despite being faced with problems like seized fixings, stripping the car down to a bare shell is comparatively easy, and there is a great temptation to rush this part of the restoration – in the process, losing track of where components are stored and even forgetting where (and which way around) some of them fit on the car! Far better to take your time and clean everything which comes off the car, catalogue and store spares in a logical order so that they can be found again.

The author also recommends that you photograph every part of the car before stripping away components, to act as an aid to memory when the time comes to re-fit them. It is surprisingly easy to forget where some small bracket fits, or which precise route a cable or length of brake pipe should follow. If you have colour photographs there should be no such problems.

Store components which are to be re-used in dry conditions, because the time interval between stripping and rebuilding can turn out to be many times longer than your initial estimate and there's little more depressing than finding the next component to be re-fitted has rusted to the point of being useless. Keep small items such as nuts and bolts in freezer bags, which can be sealed to keep out moisture and which have a panel on which you can write a description of the components inside. Any non-metal components (leather, plastics, vinyl) should be kept safe from rodent attack!

It is worthwhile slowing down the stripdown process and taking the time to separate the components into three groups. The first contains items which, with no more than cleaning, can be re-used, the second those on which some DIY reconditioning work is needed and the third comprises items which will have to be replaced.

Working slowly and methodically, taking time to sort and catalogue spares and pho-

If you can beg or borrow a spot welder then do so, it allows distortion-free welding of vulnerable panels like this Midget bonnet.

tographing everything might at first sight appear to be unnecessarily time-consuming but, unless you are fully familiar with the mechanical, electrical, trim and hydraulic components of the MGB, the extra time you spend working in this way now can save you far more time later on when you come to rebuild the car!

BODYWORK

Contrary to the published opinions of some commentators, obtaining consistently strong and neat MiG or gas welds is not easy, and comparatively few DIY restorers appear to carry out welded repairs to their own cars, sensibly bringing in a mobile welder.

As with painting, the application of the weld or paint takes little time in comparison with that needed for preparation. You could, for instance, spend a month or more cutting out rot, cleaning edges (which are to be welded) back to bright steel, tailoring repair panels and preparing them for welding, and then bring in a mobile welder who can weld the lot up in a few hours.

A mobile welder will charge by the hour, and perhaps have a standing 'call-out' charge. The

Mig welding is anything but easy! On long runs in the centre of a non-structural large panel like this Midget bonnet, tack it at perhaps 1" intervals rather than try to continuous seam weld it – not only will this reduce the chances of burning through, but it also lessens the possibility of heat rivelling being caused. See those sparks? They are molten metal which will burn through adjacent paintwork if you don't protect it. It's no fun getting one of these fellows inside your shoe, either, so wear stout leather boots when Mig welding.

hourly labour rate should be a fraction of that charged by a restoration company to carry out the same work on its own premises, and so great savings are possible.

The most important aspect of structural bodywork repair is to ensure that the bodyshell is not in the least distorted before new metal is welded on. Obvious though that may appear, it is far from unknown for restored cars to 'crab' to some extent when underway because the bodyshell was not correctly supported when the sills were welded on! In the absence of a jig, you have to resort to endless measuring to ensure that dimensions are the same either side of the car and checking levels using a spirit level.

When the bodyshell *is* level, it pays to support the main structural members so solidly that nothing short of a direct hit from a field gun can shift anything. This not only guards

against workshop visitors who appear incapable of supporting their own weight and always choose the weakest part of the bodyshell to lean on and sit on, but also guards against accidents – for instance, if you stumble, you tend to put your hand out instinctively to check your fall, and if the shell is in the way it can suffer if not properly supported.

Ideally, the front chassis rails would be supported at the front and near the rear ends, the main crossmember would have supports. The rear end of the transmission tunnel would have a flat support which spread the load and the rear chassis rails two supports apiece.

Many restorers weld braces across the door apertures before cutting away rotten metal, and this is good practice. Even better would be an internal body jig which could be securely bolted to the door hinge captive nuts, seat belt mountings and so on. Not only would such a jig make the bodyshell rigid even after the sills had been cut away, it could incorporate bolt-on arms to help correctly position repair panels. No such jig is available at the time of writing, though. At the author's suggestion at least one large organisation is studying the feasibility of manufacturing them.

However carefully you measure and support the bodyshell (and most especially the Roadster), it is essential to keep checking for accuracy by offering adjacent panels into position – for instance, temporarily fitting the doors and the front wings to check shut lines before welding the sills into position.

When fitting a repair panel, don't fit the entire panel if you don't have to, but cut it down to the smallest practicable size which still allows you to weld to strong metal. Welded repair panels always rot out firstly along the welded seam, so that when you have to repeat the repair you can still use a standard repair panel rather than the full panel. If you cut down a quarter repair panel, when you repeat the repair in years to come you can still use a repair panel rather than a half or full wing.

Lead loading. OK, it's not an MGB but it IS an MG – the author's 1974 Midget – shown here to demonstrate the dark art of lead loading. The first step is to clean the steel bright using a 40 grit disc – which also helps to key the surface and give the lead something to hold on to. Solder paint is then brushed on, heated and wiped to give a thin 'tinning' layer to which further lead can be applied. The lead is heated to a putty consistency and applied to the surface. The lumps of lead on the surface are then heated and spread – ideally with the proper spatula but in this case with an old scrap of wood.

Never sand lead using a high speed disc. This is a 40 grit disc being used at a very slow speed so that no lead enters the atmosphere to be breathed in. The dust mask is a sensible safety precaution.

PAINTWORK

Disaster seems to have a habit of striking the moment a spray gun is pointed at a car. Even experienced professionals in well-equipped paint shops who follow the text book to the letter seem to have occasional catastrophes, let alone the majority of us DIY'ers who operate in draughty damp sheds and whose paintwork problems are generally of our own making.

Most written works on automotive paintwork contain very little of relevance to the DIY enthusiast, but describe painting under ideal conditions in a fairytale fashion which the embittered amateur with an unfortunate wealth of empirical experience might harshly regard as glib. Read all you like on the subject but, like riding a bike, swimming or MiG welding without blasting holes in panels, the only real teacher is experience, usually bad.

The key to surviving car painting is recognising when to Walk Away And Leave It. Those who are foolish enough to spray cellulose without wearing the appropriate respiratory gear are most at risk in this respect – spaced-out on thinner fumes, they compound problems which, if left to their own devices, can simply disappear.

Paint runs are an obvious example. If left alone to dry, lesser runs can disappear completely (especially if the paint is cellulose) and larger runs can quite easily be flatted out with 1000 grit wet 'n dry and the surface lightly cut after the paint has cured. Yet the amateur who finds himself gazing at a solitary run can, in trying to mop up the surplus with an artist's paintbrush or a rag, contaminate the paint or even damage the underlying coats if thinners have sufficiently softened them. Walk Away And Leave It.

The second survival hint for painting is not to be careless. A friend of the author's with a lifetime of experience of paint spraying cars once inadvertently thinned his cellulose paint with brake fluid – which had been 'temporarily' stored in an empty thinners tin. This is not a good idea, and the following day the still-tacky paint had to be stripped off and it was back to Square One. The same person sprayed a large panel on which paint stripper had been used nearly a year before, and found streaks of wet paint where traces of stripper remained – he now thoroughly washes all panels before painting them. The author has spot-primed areas and neglected to flat the surrounding area of dry spray at it edges before applying the topcoats. When this was subsequently flatted, the dry spray broke through as thousands of tiny grey spots.

Before spraying paint – whether it's primer or the final topcoat – set out everything you're going to need and check that you're using the correct paint and thinners, that the spray gun is spotlessly clean inside and out, that the surface to be painted is free of finger prints, dead insects and the like, that you have clean tack rags and clean rags for the spirit wipe. You could even usefully draw up a list of jobs to be tackled (arranged into the correct order) and

materials to be used, and pin this to the workshop wall.

And the very best of luck.

BOXING UP

The final part of a restoration is the boxing up, the re-fitting of trim and mechanical components to the bodyshell. In theory, this should be the easiest and by far the most enjoyable part of the restoration if for no other reason than because it's the Home Straight and the end of the restoration is in sight.

In practice, boxing up is rarely straightforward. New or reconditioned components may not fit because they are for the wrong year of car; soft, fresh paintwork can so easily be damaged if you are the least bit careless; electrical components might not function or the engine might refuse to start due to a fuel delivery or ignition problem if you're lucky, or something more fundamental such as an out-of-timing camshaft if you're not.

Whether you have fitted a new loom or not, electrical problems can drive you to distraction. When you come to reconnect the battery, ensure that everything is switched 'off' then attach the live terminal and momentarily touch the earth terminal to its post. If you see and hear a spark at the post then something is leaking to earth, and the battery should on no account be connected until you have traced the fault – otherwise, you could start an electrical fire.

You have the option of physically going over the entire wiring system trying to locate the fault visually, which is not always possible, or using a multi-meter to trace the fault. With the battery disconnected and the multi-meter set to measure resistance (the scale which registers ohms), connect one of the multi-meter terminals to earth (the bodywork) and begin tracing the fault at the fuse block. Remove each fuse and touch the other terminal of the multi-meter against each fuse mount. When you find the one which offers low resistance, use a wiring diagram to trace the individual circuits which are connected with the fuse, and check the terminals until you locate the one causing the problem. If you cannot trace the fault then bring in a mobile auto-electrician who can.

Always think two or three jobs ahead. It is unfortunately very easy to approach a sequence of tasks in such a way that you have to remove the first component which you fitted in order to be able to fit the last! Referring to your photographic record of the initial stripdown is a great aid in avoiding this.

The author prefers not to set a deadline for the rebuild, so that he works at his own pace and avoids forcing errors which might be brought about by racing against the clock; the MOT is not booked until the car is finished and fully tested – avoiding all-night fault tracing sessions which can otherwise see the restorer bleary-eyed and anything but bushy-tailed the following morning at the MOT testing station.

But when you have restored an MGB and are rewarded for your efforts with an MOT certificate, you will feel a sense of satisfaction which few achieve.

If you suspect that your funds are about to run too low to be able to finish the restoration, try to concentrate your spending on the essentials rather than the cosmetics. Get the braking system 100% sound rather than blow the money on a shiny new rear bumper! If money is tight, leave ordering expensive items of trim until last, so that all of your available funds go into the important areas. Unfortunately, not everyone gets their priorities right in this respect and, as a result, there are a great many beautiful looking but less than roadworthy restored cars around.

If, like so many people, your funds do run out before the car is roadworthy, spend your last few pennies on a dustsheet and laid-up insurance. A part-completed restoration project car is next to worthless but, if you are pre-

pared to put the project on hold until funds permit its completion, you will eventually end up with a valuable asset.

PRO-AM RESTORATIONS

Relatively few restorations can claim to be truly 'DIY'; most people bring in some degree of professional help. Leaving aside the vanity which leads people to claim to have personally carried out restorations when in fact quite often the bulk of the work was contracted out, this is the most sensible route to a sound and roadworthy restored car.

We have already established that the majority of the work in a restoration is unskilled cleaning and scraping – the sort of work anyone can do and not to be entrusted to an over-qualified professional workshop at something frightening per hour! It is worth paying the going rate to have the relatively small amount of highly skilled work in a restoration carried out professionally to an agreed standard.

The most obvious such saving is made by undertaking the initial stripdown at home, delivering the shell to a restorer for welded repairs and spraying, then finally rebuilding the car at home afterwards. You should be rewarded with a substantial reduction in the bill, but you must be warned that the chances are you'll seriously underestimate the amount of work you are letting yourself in for and the length of time the build-up will take. Disputes between you and the restorer are quite likely to arise when you discover a scratch in the paintwork which you are sure you are not responsible for, and for which the restorer accepts no liability.

Another form of pro-am restoration is for you to strip down the car and to contract out various parts of the restoration to specialist companies to complete on their own premises – one for welded repair, another for paintwork (you can save a small fortune by doing the paint prep. yourself), and finally another for the build-up. Although the vast bulk of the restoration is carried out by professionals, you should achieve a worthwhile overall saving by virtue of the fact that you can select the most appropriate (fastest) company for each individual aspect of the restoration. The problem with this form of 'managed' restoration is that each specialist will blame the other if anything goes wrong, and it can prove nigh-on impossible to pin the blame on any of them.

The most cost-effective pro-am restoration which brings the greatest savings of all is to keep the car at your home throughout and to bring mobile specialists in to carry out the various jobs on your premises. The benefits are that you get a top-quality job at the lowest price, that you remain in full charge throughout, and that you yourself only carry out those jobs with which you're entirely comfortable. The negative aspect is that the restoration can easily turn into a full-time occupation for you – and you'll be working for no wages!

The aluminium of the MGBs bonnet is obviously much softer than the steel of the rest of the car, easily scored by abrasive materials, and paint stripper is the least destructive option when you have to strip off old paint.

CASE HISTORY –
GDG 803D

My 1966 MGB GT had been in constant daily use for over six years – apart from a few weeks off the road while various aspects of its on-going 'rolling' restoration such as sill replacement and sundry welded repairs at the rear end of the car were undertaken. Six years is approaching the expected total life-span of some of today's cars, and so it is not surprising that the car was looking generally a little down at heel. I had recently re-sprayed the aluminium bonnet which, when topcoated and re-fitted to the car, would have made the rest of the bodywork look even more shabby in comparison, and so a semi-restoration – a re-spray and general smartening-up – appeared to be the only sensible option.

Although the paintwork was dull, and despite there being a few small areas where evidence of light surface rusting was visible under

Dents in the leading edge were gently beaten until they were shallow, the aluminium was deliberately scored with 40 grit production paper to give the filler something to grip on to, and thin layers of filler were applied.

the paint (predictably, the rear wing fillets, the doors' lower regions and the front valance), the bodyshell in general was in excellent condition and very sound. Essential repairs to structural pressings and assemblies had been attended to as and when required over the years, and the underside had been taken back to bare metal and treated to Bonda-Prima followed by

Spraying an engine bay entails removing one heck of a lot of componentry. Start with the radiator and its diaphragm. Drain the coolant, drain the engine oil and that's the really messy bit over. Unbolt the coolant hoses and feed them back through the diaphragm (flush out the oil radiator while it's off the car). Undo the top and bottom hose clips, and pull the hose ends from the radiator, then unbolt the radiator stays. Either undo the diaphragm bolts and lift the whole assembly out or undo the six radiator fixing bolts and remove this, followed by the diaphragm. This job does not take long, but it appears that you have achieved quite a lot – makes you feel good and impresses onlookers.

Master cylinder stripped. It is very easy to fit a new seal set to a master cylinder – getting it out of the assembly on the scuttle of early MGBs is the problem – expect nuts and bolts to be seized. The only 'special tool' you'll need is circlip pliers. DO make sure that the circlip really is located in its ring before re-fitting the assembly to the car. If the bores of any of the master or slave cylinders show light pitting, this should be honed out using a small three-stone honer available from good motor factors – they fit in an electric drill chuck and cost very little.

cellulose and fresh underseal two years before. The only major area of the body which had not received attention during my ownership of the car (and which desperately needed it) was the engine bay.

The under-bonnet area lets down many a classic with smart and some with superb external paintwork, the problem being that the owners balk at the amount of work involved in preparing the engine bay for a respray. It's not just a simple matter of heaving the engine out; it's the myriad of electrical and mechanical components which are attached to the flitch and scuttle panels; the loom, the brake and

clutch hydraulic components, the heater, radiator and so on. The ideal opportunity to paint an engine bay thus normally presents itself only during a full restoration, when these components have been removed from the car.

Removing, cleaning, reconditioning or renewing under-bonnet components as necessary, then reassembling the lot after the paintwork has been attended to takes a lot of hard work, not a little organisation and is, in fact, tantamount to a front-end restoration. Apart from any other consideration, there will be dozens of fastenings to be removed and carefully stored away so that each can be found

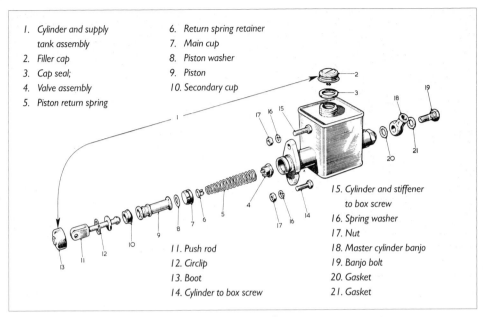

1. Cylinder and supply tank assembly
2. Filler cap
3. Cap seal;
4. Valve assembly
5. Piston return spring
6. Return spring retainer
7. Main cup
8. Piston washer
9. Piston
10. Secondary cup

11. Push rod
12. Circlip
13. Boot
14. Cylinder to box screw

15. Cylinder and stiffener to box screw
16. Spring washer
17. Nut
18. Master cylinder banjo
19. Banjo bolt
20. Gasket
21. Gasket

If you remove the master cylinder banjo, renew the two washers. Stripping the unit entails removing the circlip (12) and pulling away the push rod assembly (11). The force of the spring should then push the piston assembly forwards. Obtain a seal kit, which includes all seals, and lubricate each with a little brake fluid before reassembly. (Courtesy Autodata.)

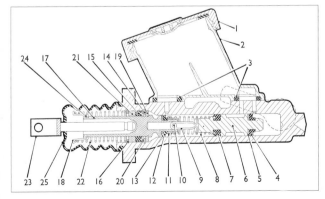

1. Filler cap
2. Plastic reservoir
3. Reservoir seals
4. Main cup
5. Piston washer
6. Piston
7. Main cup
8. Spring
9. Piston link
10. Pin
11. Pin retainer
12. Main cup
13. Piston washer
14. Circlip
15. Cup
16. Circlip
17. Piston
18. Spring retainer
19. Stop washer
20. Washer
21. Bearing
22. Spring
23. Pushrod
24. Spirolux ring
25. Rubber boot

The later master cylinders are tandem; that is, they have two pistons and two cylinders (along a common axis) which serve in effect two separate braking circuits. Any good workshop manual should contain details for overhauling these units. (Courtesy Autodata).

when needed during reassembly; fail to do this and you can waste countless hours rummaging through boxes of nuts and bolts trying to find the right one for a particular component. An external respray – although hard work – is really quite straightforward in comparison, so it's little wonder that so many owners of smart-looking classic cars hide their scruffy engine bay from prying eyes.

It's surprising just how many other jobs you can find when you begin to seriously appraise a car prior to this sort of work – jobs which you may have long intended to 'get around to doing' but for some reason never seem to have found the time for. On my car, the radiator and the clutch master cylinder both had minor leaks, the head gasket needed replacing, the wiring loom which had been 'temporarily' repaired following an electrical fire some years before needed to be replaced with the new one which had been languishing in the garage for three years, and a host of other mechanical and electrical components were also in need of some attention. In the main, most components could simply be cleaned, painted where applicable and re-fitted – even so, there are a lot of components and it's a lot of work.

Furthermore, there are many extra jobs which might not be necessary but which you will decide to carry out while access to the components concerned is good. It would be foolish, for instance, not to take the opportunity to renew the brake and clutch master cylinder seals whilst they were both off the car. As the job progresses, you tend to keep finding other little areas in need of attention.

As ever, the first job was to disconnect the battery – earth terminal first. My car originally had two six volt batteries (three cells each), wired in series so that in effect they were a six cell unit delivering twelve volts but, at some point, a previous owner had fitted in place a single 12V battery. Even though batteries have become far more efficient – smaller yet with greater storage capacity – since my MGB was

built, it is difficult to find a 12V battery which is small enough to fit in one of the two compartments but which has the necessary amp hour rating and, because the charge from the dynamo is nothing like as great as that from the later alternator, the battery does tend to run down during the winter months when the heater and lights are used a lot.

With the car off the road I had the ideal opportunity to replace the 12V battery with two 6V units. It is also a good idea to take the opportunity to fit a battery isolation switch. The list of jobs and necessary spares grows.

First off came the lights and grille. The grille itself had several badly-damaged slats and, economy being the name of the game, these were straightened rather than replaced. If the chrome is really bad and the thought of blowing nearly £100($140) on a new grille fails to thrill you, the slat assembly is available separately at quite reasonable cost. You can fit this using pop-rivets but, in the interests of good taste, cold riveting is preferable. I prefer to keep original equipment on my car wherever possible, and hence the decision to repair as best I could the grille slats. To straighten the damaged slats, I cut a small piece of softwood to length, then whittled and sanded it until it was a tight fit in an undamaged slat. This was then pressed into each bent slat in turn, and padded pliers were used to tease the slat back into its 'V' shape. The repaired grille is still far from perfect, but perhaps because of this it looks entirely in place on the twenty-seven year-old car.

The carburettors and their linkages were removed complete. The carbs had fairly recently been overhauled (new jets and needles), and so they merely needed external cleaning. Normally, if you remove carburettors which have not received attention for some time, you would be well advised to clean sediment out of the fuel bowls, and to replace the fuel bowl needles plus the main needles and jets. The jets will then have to be centred, and

MG engine bay stripped. You passed the real Point Of No Return when you cut out the old loom; it's no good looking at the now denuded engine bay and thinking "What have I let myself in for?" Think positive. You're about to enter one of the most trying periods of your life.

Salvage from loom. Don't throw it away! Salvage any good steel from cut out panels, wires and connectors from old looms – you never know when they may come in handy.

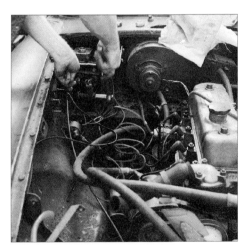

Master cylinder removal. Bleed both cylinders dry. The brake/clutch master cylinder assembly can be a pig to remove. The collection of $7/_{16}$" bolts with one $1/_2$" mysterious interloper holding the cover in place is anything but easy to get a socket to, leaving you worrying about how on earth you're going to get them back in. Don't worry, they're not too bad. Disconnect the pedal return springs, then remove the pivot bolt and the pedal pivot split pins. The cylinders can now be removed after you have unbolted the banjo connectors.

Heater return valve. Check here for leakage; the return valve is also a common cause of poor heater performance; not because of any problem with the valve itself, but because previous owners fit the valve using 'liquid' gaskets. The heat from the coolant melts this and it forms a partial chewing gum-like diaphragm across the block inlet.

any workshop manual will describe this simple process. On older SU carburettors, the main butterfly spindle may be the source of air induction and, if this is suspected (spray a little carburettor lubricant onto the spindle ends; if this temporarily cures the problem then the leakage is proven), it would be worth taking the opportunity to have bushes fitted or obtain exchange reconditioned carbs.

Next, the coolant and engine oil were drained in order that the radiator and its surround could be removed. The oil cooler radiator was unbolted and held aloft for a minute or so while its oil drained back into the block, before the pipes were disconnected and threaded back through the radiator surround. The radiator and its surround could then be unbolted and lifted away. The oil cooler radiator contained some fairly unpleasant-looking black sludge which was flushed out using diesel oil. The unit was then filled with clean engine oil to prevent internal corrosion whilst it was off the car.

Now came the Point Of No Return – removal of the old loom, itself a daunting process. Each wire end was cut to leave a short length of wire and its spade connector on each terminal, to make the fitting of the new loom easier. The new loom itself already sported a large number of folded masking tape tags, on each of which I had previously written the names of the component associated with the individual wire. This was to some extent to speed the fitting, but mainly to ensure that the loom was the right one for the car before it was half-fitted! Checking a loom in this way is not too difficult. Lay it out, preferably on a table, alongside the car so that the positions of the terminals roughly correspond to the areas of the car where they will be fitted. It is now possible to identify individual wires on the loom by comparison with those which you can see on the car, cross-referencing with a wiring diagram just in case anyone has previously 'customised' the wiring! As each wire is identified,

make up a folded tag of masking tape and write on it the name of the component to which the wire runs. As more and more wires are tagged, a process of elimination makes identification of the remainder that much easier.

The loom itself has three components; the main body runs between the dashboard and the engine bay, a separate smaller loom runs from the engine bay to the rear of the car and a third small loom is for the overdrive. Many people are daunted by the prospect of rewiring a car but, once the loom is roughly in position, with the help of a wiring diagram it's not that difficult a task, and you can always summon assistance from an auto electrician if you do get stuck. The most important point is to have someone on hand to immediately disconnect the battery earth connection if anything appears amiss when you test the electrics on re-assembly.

With the loom pushed back into the cab, the next two large items to be removed from the engine bay were the brake/clutch master cylinder assembly and the heater. Neither proved the slightest bit co-operative. The master cylinders' cover had previously been removed and re-painted, and so none of the self-tappers gave any problems, though it is usual to have to drill these out. The master cylinders are held in a fabrication which, on my car, is fastened to the scuttle and the bulkhead by nine bolts with $7/16"$ heads and one with a $1/2"$ head. Before tackling these, bleed both hydraulic systems and then remove the split pins from the pedal end clevis pins, and pull the pins out to free the pushrod ends. Then remove the $5/6"$ headed pedal pivot bolt, and reassemble the spacers and washers onto this for safe keeping.

The brake and clutch lines can now be removed from their respective master cylinders, though expect neither to give up without a struggle! Then and then only turn your attention to the 10 main bolts. One of the bolts through the bulkhead has a nut on the other end which holds a wiring loom clamp. so remove the nut from inside the car first. The author found that a combination of a very thin-walled $7/16"$ ($1/4"$ drive) socket fitted with a quarter to three-eights adapter and a three-eights to half inch adapter in series, then a knuckle joint followed by a 10" extension bar – was necessary to get to some of the bolt heads.

Before attempting to remove the heater, of course, drain the coolant, remove the pipes from the unit and, if the job is being carried out in isolation, disconnect the battery and part the wiring bullet connectors.

The MGB heater unit can be rather awkward to remove. Firstly, the five Philips-headed set screws along the lower rim usually distort and have to be drilled out. There being insufficient room to get an electric drill anywhere near these, the author resorted to using the drill with a flexible drive shaft. The remains of the heads were then chiselled off. These would have to be replaced with self-tapping hexagon headed screws, because the original set screws ran into captive nuts, and their threads were seized solid.

From inside the car, remove the ashtray and pull the speaker panel out far enough for the speaker wires to be disconnected, then remove the panel. Use a stubby screwdriver to undo the four self-tapping screws which hold the heater outlet seal plate (with the demister elbows sticking out) onto the bulkhead, slacken one of the hose clamps, remove that hose and pull the assembly out of the way.

The heater cab/screen control cable is affixed to the bottom of the heater unit by two bolts which can be seen through the outlet plate aperture (use a torch) when the heater assembly is raised slightly (you'll probably have to break the seal to get it to move). The $5/16"$ headed bolt on the cable outer clamp can just be reached though the aperture. To slacken the $1/4"$ head bolt which holds the cable inner, use a socket with a 10" extension bar, offered through the driver's side footwell air outlet. Pull the cable away. The heater unit may now be lifted out. When you come to re-fit the

heater unit, it is suggested that you connect the cable firstly and feed the end of this through the grommet into the car before lowering the heater into position – it's a real pain trying to fit the cable end once the heater is in situ.

The scuttle on the offside of the car had some areas of very soft paint where someone (surely not the author?) had spilt hydraulic fluid, a few small areas of sound paint but, in the main, surface rusting. Fortunately, all of

Paint stripper. Using 40 grit production paper discs in an electric drill with sanding attachment removed most of the flitch panel (engine bay side) paint, but the myriad of nooks and crannies begged to be given a taste of the paint stripper. This is disgusting stuff: given half a chance it will burn though the outer layers of your skin and get to work on the nerve endings – wear disposable gloves, a long-sleeved garment, goggles (who knows what it would do to your eyes), and keep a bucket of water handy for washing tortured limbs and digits. Don't leave any trace of stripper on bare steel; it will rust it more effectively than a week in a seaside car park.

97

the metal was still strong, and so loose rust and sundry gunge was scraped away before the scuttle was taken back to bright steel with coarse emery. The nearside scuttle had recently been cleaned back and hand painted, but this too was taken back to bare steel in order that the whole engine bay could be painted in one go and, hopefully, all end up in the same colour.

The last step in clearing the engine bay ready for its respray was removal of the steering column, accomplished by undoing the bolts on the universal joint and pulling the steering wheel back into the cab. I did consider taking the rack off as well, but decided that I could work around the lower portion of the column.

Rather than risk injuring my back removing the heavy B series engine (although my neighbour – a farmer – did offer the use of his tractor and forks, which I deemed too imprecise a lifting method, very liable to damage the first motion shaft), I elected to mask it by the simple expedient of pulling a dustbin liner over it. These are also useful for masking wheels, but it is essential that they are replaced (or turned inside-out) after each coat of paint goes on. Paint which lands on the bin liners dries but does not adhere, and if you spray on further layers of paint then the dust from the liners will be kicked into the atmosphere. As an alternative, use discarded old cotton and wool clothing, curtains and the like, all of which can be washed after use ready for the next time.

With the flitch panels and scuttle cleared of components, wires and brake/clutch lines, I began removing the old paint. Synstrip paint stripper was used on the larger panels, starting at the top and working downwards. Frequent use of an old cylinder vacuum cleaner to remove the sodden paint from the engine bay sides and chassis legs allowed me to see more clearly which areas remained to be done.

Flat and convex areas were tackled using a 40 grit disc in an electric drill at a slow speed because this removes paint very quickly and it

Spray outfit. "I was amazed". " It really works!". Spiel which normally accompanies advertised testimonials to washing powders is true of HVLP spray equipment. The alternative is small tank compressor (STC for short) spraying which, in the considerable (unfortunately) experience of the author, is about as useful as mittens on a rocking horse. STC spraying means oil and water droplets in your expensive paint spray, motors which overheat and cut out when you are 50% of the way across a large panel, noise, bounce-back and huge paint wastage. Meet the Apollo 400 – the puny member of the HVLP family – I'd happily spray a lorry with it. No contamination, less paint wastage, runs all day without having to stop to catch its breath – and it is very quiet, sounds so deceptively like a vacuum cleaner that my neighbours think I have the cleanest classic in Christendom. It's a shame that I didn't buy the Apollo until after I had finished this onerous respray!

also deals with any underlying rust traces at the same time. Also used were a selection of scrapers, wire brushes and flap wheels, each of which is ideally suited to specific areas. In awkward corners the paint was simply scraped away using old screwdrivers and chisels, and even one-off scrapers fashioned from steel bar to suit some particular nook or cranny.

The scuttle still showed some small areas of pitting which contained rust, and no amount of wire brushing or sanding seemed to shift it. A cup brush fitted in my electric angle grinder did the trick, and also proved useful for cleaning some convex panels.

The areas on which paint stripper had been used slowly turned brown from the action of stripper which remained on the surface, and this was largely cleaned off by hand using 240 grit abrasive papers. The alternative would have been to wash off any remaining stripper as soon as the paint had been removed, but the difficulties of drying the myriad of nooks and crannies in the engine bay in order to prevent immediate rusting ruled this out.

The bonnet slam panel and − for some unfathomable reason − the radiator support panel underneath had a dent apiece. These were dealt with by firstly beating each out as far as possible, then filling using P38, which was hand-blocked flat.

The paint stripping and rust removal took four full days. I have always counselled would-be restorers that the bulk of restoration is concerned with such cleaning and that actual welding, panel beating and mechanical repair − which is how restoration is usually depicted − is a tiny part of the work entailed. Another aspect which is rarely described is the personal injuries which you are likely to receive; I counted ten small wounds and a blood blister on my hands following the four days' stripping and cleaning.

I decided to use Tractol corrosion-resisting primer paint, which costs far less than similar products sold for automotive use. Although this is not generally found in the automotive world (try your nearest agricultural engineers' supplies business), it is an excellent product which can be over-coated with any paint type except two-pack. It is far from easy to spray the lower regions of the flitch panels with the engine still in situ, but it is not impossible. Unfortunately, I decided to over-thin the paint (to allow low-pressure spraying and hopefully less wastage and potential for over-spray) which gave it almost the viscosity of water.

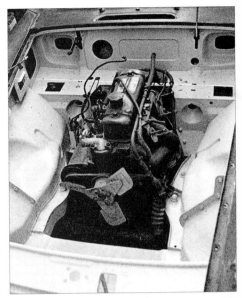

MG engine bay in primer. Primer always looks good − unless you have sprayed it over traces of paint stripper or incompatible paint types, that is. Bring on the wet 'n dry 1000 grit with lots of water, several pints of elbow grease and you'll eventually have a surface ready for topcoating.

The error was not apparent until I had nearly finished when pools of paint at the rear chassis leg tops and a lot of visible runs on the flitch panels made my mistake obvious. However, as the thinners evaporated, some of the runs disappeared.

You can over spray Tractol within thirty minutes but, as usual, I elected to leave it alone to harden for a week (a looming week's holiday helped make the decision easier). During this time, the paint would hopefully harden properly, so that it would stand less chance of it reacting with the cellulose thinners in the filler primer which was to follow. A straight softening of the Tractol by cellulose thinners would probably not in itself have caused any adverse effects, but could have resulted in the

MG engine bay in topcoat – engine covered.
Looking good. The engine bay, along with the interior and the boot space, are not so critical regarding the excellence of the final finish as the external surfaces of the car. In fact, you can get away with murder so long as the interior is the right colour. Always stir the paint thoroughly before thinning to achieve this uniformity of colour.

Poor masking. One problem with painting a car piecemeal is the chances of your masking tape covering an area of primer like this. Rather than risk masking the soft new surrounding paint, use an artists' brush to paint small areas like this.

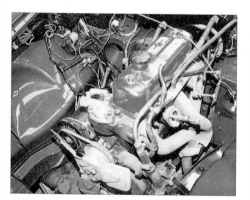

MG engine bay in topcoat. The longer you can leave the paint to harden before you begin boxing up the better; it is all to easy to damage soft cellulose. Try to work more slowly and methodically than normal, to minimise the chances of scratching the new paint; use ring spanners rather than open enders.

The same goes for scratches. Don't mess around attempting to feather the edges of a scratch in soft paint; you'll get into all sorts of trouble. Use a brush. Provided that you get a sufficient thickness of paint on, it can always be cut back at a later date to give a good finish.

thinners getting at any tiny remaining traces of oils or incompatible paint types underneath the primer.

A week later I examined the paint closely

and decided that I could not live with the runs, which were taken out using coarse emery, unfortunately revealing some bare patches of steel, which I degreased then sprayed with

Tractol. Then it was time to spray on the filler primer.

Above all, I wanted a good depth of filler primer so that I would be able to flat the rather complicated contours of the flitch without fear of going back to the Tractol – or worse – the bare steel. Thus I used rather less thinners than normal, and sprayed at a higher pressure, giving the bay three coats. Then it was 'walk away and leave it' time – a week for the paint to harden before I began flatting it ready for the cellulose topcoats. In the interim, I decided to amuse myself by dealing with the under-dash wiring.

Dashboard removal on the MGB GT is, to put it mildly, awkward. At either end, the dash is held by a half inch nut running onto a fixed stud, and these are relatively painlessly removed (though murder to get back on) using a socket and extension bar. Also easy to get at are the self-tappers which hold the glove compartment, and the two bolts in the central underside. The steering column bolt should be removed, and the column can then be pulled down out of the way. The problem fixings are two bolts situated above the speedometer and tachometer, which run into captive nuts in a bracket on the scuttle. To improve access, remove the tachometer, and you will be able to get a small 3/8" ratchet drive onto the bolt heads.

The wiring behind the dash was a real mess. Some years previously, an electrical fire caused by an uninsulated feed wire spade connector had worked its way loose and shorted to earth, resulting in damage to a number of wires both behind the dash and in the engine bay. I had replaced the damaged wire as best I could, but with the dash removed I found other wiring which was damaged but not replaced. One such wire was red and hence part of the (unfused) lighting circuit – I have been lucky not to have a second electrical fire!

An unexpected sunny (though none too warm) day provided me with the opportunity

to get the under-bonnet area topcoated. The filler primer had been sprayed on a week earlier, and so it had hardened sufficiently for me to be able to flat the surface with 1000 grit used

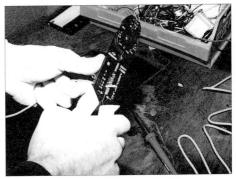

Soldering wires – stripped and twisted. Another basic skill is soldering – it's easy if you do it properly. Firstly, strip the ends of the wire(s) and twist the strands together.

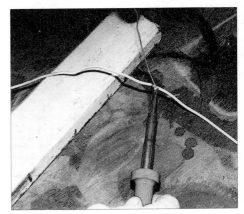

Soldering wires – solder being applied. Then apply heat to the far side of the wire as the solder is fed in. The heat and flux conspire to draw the molten solder deep into the joint. The only drawback with soldering joints is that the heat does make wire susceptible to work hardening but, if you apply heat shrink wrap insulation afterwards, this should help support the joint and act as a shock absorber, so that it won't work harden on the worst boneshaker.

wet, de-grease and paint. As this was October, any potential paint spray day presented an opportunity not to be missed!

I had no less than four part-used tins of BU09 Mineral Blue cellulose left over from the car's previous respray some years ago which, it must be admitted, had been a rushed affair and none too successful. I poured all of the paint into one large tin, mixed it thoroughly, then poured it back into two 2-litre tins. After cleaning out the inside of the largest tin and removing the rust and dust, I stretched a piece of stocking over the top and used this to filter the paint – removing all sorts of nasties. Cellulose seems to have a very long – almost indefinite – shelf life, and it's worth keeping any surplus paint after you have been spraying.

As it happened, I ordered more cellulose from Bancrofts but did not need even all of the paint which I already had in stock! My next restoration project car – probably a Morris Minor or perhaps another MG Midget – will probably hence be finished in 'wrong' Mineral Blue [it IS a Minor and it IS Mineral Blue – final edit, Autumn 1994]. It would, thinking about it, be pretty neat to have a set of matching classic cars!

It is far from easy to spray an engine bay with the engine in situ because of restricted gun movement (a gravity-fed gun would give easier access), but I found that if I sprayed under the flitch top rim first, then the chassis legs and flitch lower quarters, the rest was easy. I gave the engine bay five coats with 20 minute intervals in between, then placed the (still in primer) bonnet on top to keep out dirt.

A few days later, I decided to topcoat the bonnet. This was firstly hand-blocked with 1000 grit wet 'n dry, de-greased and given a wipe with a tack rag before four coats of cellulose were applied at twenty minute intervals. Although the bonnet when viewed from more than a couple of feet away looked fine, under close inspection, it shows many minor blemishes in the paint preparation. This is the dif-

ference between normal restoration and concourse. Had I been aiming for a concourse finish then the topcoats would have been re-flatted and more applied until the surface was perfect.

Then it was time to begin fitting the new loom inside the car. The new loom was tape bound and, whilst this does sacrifice authenticity to some extent, it is longer-lasting and cheaper to buy than fabric bound versions.

Firstly, I cut old wires from the various switches and components under the dashboard – inadvertently cutting through two of the dashboard illumination wires, which should be retained! These were soldered back together and covered with heat-shrink insulation. The old loom was reluctant to come out and took a deal of persuasion – the new loom was equally reluctant to go in, but with patience, the loom was fastened to the bulkhead and the wiring-up could begin. Even with short lengths of wire on all of the connectors and the majority of the wires on the new loom tagged, I still had to refer to the circuit diagram more than once to confirm what went where – there's a lot of wiring under a dashboard!

In the engine bay, there seemed no logical way to route the various branches of the looms (the MGB loom is a system of up to four separate components if overdrive is fitted) and the brake/clutch pipes. I dug out an old article (in a magazine called Specialist Car) which I had written following the loom fire some years before and happily found that the article was accompanied by two colour photographs of the engine bay, which showed me exactly what went where. Most enthusiasts will not have this luxury, and the importance of taking plenty of colour photographs before stripping out the engine bay becomes obvious.

When trying to fit a replacement loom, do bear in mind that the manufacturer of the loom will in most cases make the loom up so that it fits more than one version of the car in question; my loom contained surplus wires which

Removal of the transmission tunnel cover plate allows access to the overdrive inhibitor switch – the switch which only energises the overdrive circuit when the car is in third and fourth gear. To fit a new loom with overdrive wiring you'll have to remove this cover – take the opportunity to paint or otherwise mark the car's registration number onto the underside of the cover and the gearbox. Few ringers would go to the trouble of looking for such well-hidden marks, and they could provide proof positive of ownership were your car ever to be stolen.

Clutch, bleed nipple. Bleeding the clutch slave cylinder is essentially the same as bleeding the brakes; the cylinder seal kit fits in much the same way as the master cylinder kit – consult a workshop manual if your require more details.

Clutch cylinder stripped. Stripping and repairing the clutch master cylinder is essentially the same as doing the brake master cylinder. If you feel a particular need for hand holding, any workshop manual will provide step by step instructions.

103

turned out to be reversing light wiring. This was not standardised until the Mk.2 version of the MGB (mine is a Mk.1), and I only found out what the wiring was after studying the circuit diagram for the Mk.2 car. When fitting a loom, you cannot afford to go into automatic pilot mode – you must keep your mind on the job at all times. Before fitting a wire, mentally confirm its type (feed, earth etc) and check that it is being fitted to the correct terminal – failure to do this can result in an electrical fire within minutes of reconnecting the battery – and a wrecked new loom!

Before fitting any part of a loom, study exactly where it runs and, in particular, where it passes through a bulkhead or other small gap, and fit the grommet before trying to get the loom into place. The author did not bother doing this and so began fitting the rear loom in the engine bay, then working backwards under the car. All went well until he came to a small hole through which the loom passed into the

spare wheel well and instantly realised that you have to begin at the back end of the car and work forwards – the rearmost part of the loom being far too large to feed through the hole.

The overdrive wiring includes a single wire which runs to the gearbox switch (and which only allows the overdrive to operate in third and top gears), then on to the solenoid. In order to fit this it was necessary to remove the large cover from the transmission tunnel. The most awkward part of the entire rewiring operation proved to be connecting the fuel pump.

The old loom was plundered for bullet and spade connectors and lengths of wire – most of which will one day come in useful for repairing or adding to the loom on the MG or perhaps another car with Lucas wiring conventions – which covers most BMC/BL/Austin Rover classics and which, of course will use the same colour-coding and usually wire thicknesses. The bullet connectors are particularly useful and, because they have to be soldered onto

Running a tap through a captive nut after spraying: fail to do this and the chances are that any bolt fitted will seize as the paint in the nut threads hardens. A drop of oil on the bolt thread should prevent rust from being a cause of seizure.

To clear paint from threads, a bolt of the appropriate size with a groove filed into the thread offers a cheaper alternative to buying taps and wrenches. Cutting through one flat of a nut, incidentally, gives a cheap paint-removing die!

wire, far better than the crimped alternative – in addition to being free! If you heat the connector to melt the solder within then you can pull out the old wire. To connect a new length of wire, heat the end and tin it with solder, then heat the bullet connector and push the wire into place, and put a dab of solder in the small hole at the front of the connector.

The clutch master cylinder seal kit arrived and was fitted but, when I had rebuilt the master cylinder assembly, fitted it to the car and put hydraulic fluid into the clutch cylinder, I was horrified to note that some was leaking from the banjo end fitting seals. The entire assembly did not have to come out – I managed with some difficulty to remove just the clutch cylinder – and new copper seals were obtained and fitted. It is as well to replace the banjo seals as a matter of course when you fit a new master cylinder kit! It is also worth making the switch to silicone hydraulic fluid because, if a repaired cylinder does prove to have a leak, this won't damage the new paintwork on the scuttle!

Time and time again during the re-fitting of the engine bay, work was temporarily held up due to some spare being needed. The throttle cable end was hopelessly frayed and, although it could have been fitted, sooner or later it would have jammed in its outer sleeve and left me with an open throttle – no fun, I can assure you. The two rubber seals in the rocker box cover proved to have become brittle and could not perform their duty – which is to keep any moisture including rainwater which might land on the cover when the bonnet was raised or escaping coolant – out of the rocker gear. These too were replaced.

I permitted myself the luxury of a reconditioned radiator from my local MG Spares supplier to replace the leaking, sludge-filled and damaged original. This was expensive to buy but in the long term should prevent otherwise unavoidable (and potentially VERY expensive) problems with overheating. The lower-cost

alternative to buying a reconditioned radiator is to de-solder the core and to solder in a new one – a skilled job which I did not feel competent to tackle.

The radiator turned out to have been re-cored OK, but the company which did the work appeared to have replaced three of the captive nuts which secure the radiator to its diaphragm, not only using larger nuts but also UNC rather than the correct UNF thread. Two of these were at the top of the radiator and thus have to be bolted to the radiator diaphragm stays. Not only did I have to drill both the diaphragm and stay holes oversize, but also hunt around for UNC nuts, which I eventually found by taking them off my three-legged puller. My spares dealer changed their supplier after this episode.

Another expense but one which was really avoidable was a small set of UNF taps to clean out the paint-filled threads of captive nuts within the engine bay. Fail to do this and any bolts which you fit stand an excellent chance of cracking the new paint around the fitting and are certain to prove seized solid if ever you have to remove them in the future. If you cannot afford a set of taps, then create your own paint-clearing taps by filing a groove along the threaded shank of a bolt. The groove acts as a reservoir for paint as it is screwed into its captive nut.

Most of the rubber seals within the engine bay were perished and some disintegrated when they were removed. Replacements were obtained for most of these and, whilst the replacements were fairly inexpensive, they were not as good quality as the originals. A better solution might have been to obtain some sheet rubber and cut out seals as and when needed – at a pinch, old inner tubes or an old wellington boot could have been used.

Again, the scope of the 'tidy-up' was destined to grow as I compared the shiny new paint in the engine bay and on the bonnet with the dull paintwork of the car's exterior, and concluded that there was no way I could live with the latter. A full re-spray was the only way forwards. Bodywork-wise the old GT was in rather good condition, being very sound and looking down at heel only by virtue of its paintwork. The front valance, however, had taken a real pounding on a length of deeply-rutted private driveway which had not only altered its contours but also exposed areas of steel which had duly rusted.

The first task was to beat the valance back into something resembling its original shape, accomplished with hammers and dollies. I did not waste too much time truing this panel, partly on the grounds that it's hidden away behind the front bumper (and the remaining dents would divert attention from the rust on aforesaid bumper) but mainly because, living in a rural area, I know full well that dented valances on sportscars are an inevitability.

To clean off the existing paint and rust, I opted for a 40 grit carborundum disc, used at slow revolutions in the electric drill, resisting the temptation to punish the already thinnish metal of the valance with the fierce (11,000 rpm) angle grinder, which can go through thin steel like the proverbial hot knife through butter. When the surface was free of paint and rust, I hand-brushed on one coat of Bona Prima (to deal with traces of ferrous oxide in the surface of the steel) followed by two good thick sprayed coats of stone-chip which, for the benefit of the uninitiated, forms a thick, energy-absorbing surface which should, in theory, absorb the minor impacts caused by flying stones. This was to finally be top-coated before being re-fitted on the car.

The work described so far was interspersed with bouts of cleaning sundry components and painting them with black or silver Smoothrite during idle moments. The components included the heater unit, the headlamp bowls (transformed from rusted hulks into quite smart-looking components), the radiator diaphragm (which had to be butt welded because a previous owner had cut it in two,

presumably to remove the radiator without having to unbolt its diaphragm), the clutch and brake cylinder assembly, and so on.

It must be admitted that Smoothrite is not the 'correct' paint to use on these components, and concours enthusiasts would doubtless throw up their hands in horror at the use of such an un-authentic paint, most especially on visible components such as the heater unit. However, I have found that, provided all loose rust and oils are removed from steel, Smoothrite and its hammered-finish and better known stablemate Hammerite do hold rust at bay as long as any other treatment I've ever used. So there! One point worthy of note is that both Hammerite and Smoothrite have a six week curing period.

The legacy of the burst oil cooler pipe was that most of the components were covered in a mixture of oil and dirt, which had, it must be admitted, kept rust from spreading but which had to come off before the under-bonnet components could be painted. A variety of methods were chosen, according to the size of the component. Nuts, bolts and washers were dumped for a hour or so in a bath of either paraffin or (more effectively) gun-wash thinners, the latter also dealing with any traces of paint. Larger components were cleaned using the same substances but in conjunction with either an old toothbrush, an old paintbrush or, for those 'stubborn' stains, a wire brush.

Anxious to get the engine running as soon as possible (it does them no good to lie idle for too long), I checked that none of the as-yet unconnected terminals – mainly in the lighting circuit – was earthing, and went over as many of the wiring connections as possible to make sure everything was in order before I reconnected the battery. With everything switched off, any earth problem would manifest itself as a spark when the second (earth) battery terminal was touched against its post, so that I could immediately disconnect it before any damage was done. No spark meant that I could confi-

MG roof paint stripping. Over a dozen layers of paint on the roof made stripping it back to bare metal the only sensible option – put cellulose thinners on top of such thicknesses and you might be lucky and get away with it but the usual outcome is reaction. Apart from any other consideration, scratches in the surface probably hold traces of car polish.

Filling the roof actually took several days. The filler goes on in thin layers, each of which is flatted using a block before the application of the next layer. Try to apply one thick layer of filler and it will be full of holes, which will make themselves apparent when you flat the surface. Old curtains provide some sort of overnight cover for the porous filler.

dently connect the battery and begin testing the electrics. The fuel pump burst into life as the ignition was switched on, then the wipers, heater motor and horn all proved to be in working order. The next stage was to try and run the engine.

The cylinder head having been removed, I set the valve clearances. Then I filled the radiator with coolant, the engine with oil (the bores had previously received a light coating of oil – pump a little oil through the spark plug holes then spin the engine on the starter to get the bores covered before laying up an engine for any length of time), and spun the engine (spark plugs out) for thirty or so seconds to get the oil circulating before the bottom end was subjected to a pounding when the engine was actually fired up. With the plugs and leads in situ, the engine fired but ran very roughly until I remembered that the direction of rotation of the distributor rotor arm was anti-clockwise, and reconnected numbers two and three plug leads in the right order – then she ran sweet as a nut.

Unfortunately, the bottom hose proved to be leaking and the clutch banjo connection was

still leaking brake fluid. A complete set of hoses was obtained and fitted, and the clutch master cylinder came out yet again – such is restoration.

The engine bay was then masked off while the external paint work was attended to. The roof was flatted using 1000 grit wet 'n dry, then a couple of small areas of filler spot primed – and there was massive reaction between the new primer and the underlying paint. I tried spot priming a couple of other areas and the same thing happened. The problem was that deep, if minuscule, cracks in the paint (too deep to be flatted out) held traces of car polish to which, of course, no paint would adhere and which caused the reaction when attacked by the powerful cellulose thinners.

When paint reacts in this way, you can try using a barrier coat to keep new paint away from the existing surface – but to cover an entire bodyshell is a colossal 'bodge' and simply out of the question – the old paint has to come off. Strip and clean discs proved the fastest method of getting off the old paint, but even these were still painfully slow. The reason

107

for the paint reaction soon became obvious – no less than nine layers of paint covered the roof to a thickness of a third of a millimetre.

Stripping the paint from the roof gave me the opportunity to address another little problem. At some time, it appears that someone has jumped onto the roof with such force that there has always been a pronounced circular crease in the roof for as long as I've owned the car. I removed the headlining in order to be able to get a dolly under the crease and tried to beat this out, but the steel had stretched and was having none of it. In the end I had to beat the raised area as best I could and then apply bodyfiller to solve the problem.

Applying filler, flatting and then repeating the process to lose the circle in the roof took over three weeks (partly due to the worst November snows since '63 in the UK, which took the temperature in the workshop down so far that filler took ages to harden) and, even after that time, it was far from perfect. I started off by flatting the filler using an electric random orbital sander, but eventually came to the conclusion that this was causing unwanted profiles in the filler. A length of wood used as a sanding block with 80 grit production paper proved the best method.

With the rest of the roof taken back to bare metal and thoroughly de-greased, you could reasonably expect to be able to spray on primer without any fear of reactions occurring, there simply being nothing for the new paint to react with! However, when I sprayed on the filler primer, two small areas did react; both were small arcs which followed the outline of the crease in the roof, and I can only speculate that the surface of the steel had tiny fractures which retained some contaminant – probably silicones. These small areas were flatted, given a coat of Bar Coat barrier paint and re-primed.

I had sprayed on the filler/primer wet (with a high proportion of thinners), which allowed the paint to flow well, reducing the naturally matt primer finish – which showed that my

Headlight bowl flatting. When flatting the primer on the headlamp bowl, areas of the existing paint quickly broke though the surface, indicating that the existing paintwork had a very uneven surface. In this respect, the primer was acting as a guide coat, and so it was flatted right back.

efforts with the body filler to lose the circular crease (perhaps two weeks' work) had not been entirely successful, although further building up of thin layers of cellulose putty would help.

The next step was to prepare the rest of the bodyshell for repainting. I could have opted to spot prime problem areas only before spraying on the topcoats, but reasoned that if I got the entire shell into primer then I would stand a greater chance of obtaining an even result. In the event, I was lucky to have made that choice. I flatted the paintwork until it appeared smooth, then sprayed on the first coat of primer. Just to be sure that everything was in order, I wet flatted this and was rewarded with areas where high spots in the original topcoats broke through as hundreds of tiny blue dots. This was actually the remains of dry spray which had never been cut. In this respect, the first primer coat was acting as a guide coat, and I flatted the problem areas until I was back to unbroken blue and then re-primed.

With the car in primer, I could still see some of the circular crease in the roof, and so set about losing this with cellulose body stopper, applied as a number of very thin layers which

When all traces of the primer had been flatted out, the resulting surface was then flat. This was painted again using primer, ready for flatting and topcoating.

that it was contaminated with thousands of tiny craters. I believe that the water/oil mixture which had been spitting out of the spray gun instantly spreads when it hits the painted surface, just as a drop of oil in water spreads out. In the very centre of the resultant circle is a tiny area of paint, surrounded by the oil which prevents the topcoat from adhering to the surface. The horizontal surfaces (roof, wing tops etc) were far worse than vertical surfaces.

The problem, I eventually discovered, was partially caused by the oil/water trap – attached directly to the tank outlet – not being upright, so I connected the old coiled hose from the tank outlet to the oil/water trap, which I fastened to the wall, and ran the new hose off this.

Now I could spray without the gun constantly spitting a mixture of water and oil with the paint, although the occasional drop still found its way through the system. By chance, I had ordered a quick release coupling which, I discovered, acted as a de-humidifier – for want of a better term – insofar as it appeared that any water which did make its way up the air line condensed out when it reached the cold coupling and spat out from the joint rather than from the spray gun. I wrapped a piece of cloth around the joint to keep the water from falling onto the sprayed surface and prepared to try again.

built up sufficiently to hide the crease. This was wet flatted using a block, then more primer-filler was applied over the top until the crease all but vanished.

After years of struggling with a coiled air hose on my small compressor, I ordered a 30-ft long proper hose from local suppliers. What a difference! For a start, I was able to park the compressor out of the way under a bench instead of having to drag it around the car behind me, and furthermore, to insulate the area from the sound viewpoint so that spraying operations did not disturb my neighbours. Equally importantly, the new hose did not, unlike the old, have water droplets condensing out inside it. Those plastic coiled hoses which come with cheap sets of air tools aren't worth the bother.

However, the month being January, the humidity was high and my single in-line water/oil trap failed to stop gunge comprising a mixture of water and oil from the compressor reaching the spray gun, from which it emerged as thousands of tiny droplets. The severity of this was not apparent until after I had sprayed on the first top coat, and found

The paint which I had sprayed on the car had so many small circular craters in it that I decided to wet flat the lot back to primer on the roof and all surfaces down to the waist line of the car, lower (vertical) panels seeming to have escaped the contamination. This, as it turned out, was just as well, because I found a number of runs and some very uneven areas in the primer which had previously been invisible. The lower sections of the bodywork were wet flatted until I could feel no roughness.

At this point, those creating concours cars would have sprayed on many layers of topcoat, flatting each before spraying the next but, as

Fitting the bonnet. The single-handed bonnet fit is made slightly more risky by the softness of the paint, but here goes. With plenty of padding on the scuttle and rear channel, the bonnet is carefully lowered into position, the front raised, and held using a central prop.

The nuts and bolts which secure the bonnet to its hinges are then assembled. I'm using my head to hold the bonnet in the desired position; pull the bonnet as far forwards as possible, and tighten the front fixings.

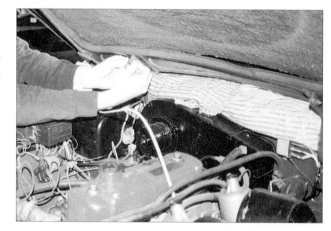

Then raise the rear of the bonnet, and fasten the rear fixings. The idea is to position the bonnet as far forwards and as high as possible at the rear edge, lessening the chances of its rear edge fouling the rear channel and scraping paint when it is trial lowered.

When you do lower the bonnet, don't be surprised if you manage to scrape some paint off the slam panel and catch mechanism. It's not the end of the world, simply brush paint out the scratch.

Cutting the paint. After a suitable period of hardening (I usually leave paintwork for six weeks or so), the paint surface can if desired be gently cut.

Polishing. Cut areas should be polished at the earliest opportunity. The new colour enriched polishes appear to work very well, and seem to be long-lasting.

my cars are all for daily use rather than show (and because I wanted to get the car back on the road), I sprayed on just two thick coats of cellulose. This was thinned using anti-bloom (fast) primers just enough so that I could see my reflection in the freshly-painted surface, giving a heavy application able to flow out but rather quick-drying so that it was not vulnerable to blooming. As the date was 1st. February and a stream of showers arriving from the West made the air quite humid, blooming could have been a real problem, and I was fortunate in choosing the right times to spray – in each case just over twenty minutes before the next rain storm!

It had been six months since I had started work on the bonnet re-spray which had led to the under-bonnet re-spray and in turn to the semi-restoration. Had the bodyshell needed welding then I could have easily doubled this time requirement, not because the welding itself would have taken another six months, but because the extra stripping out of components so that I could weld without setting fire to the car, plus the work on those components and the subsequent re-build, would have added six months to the total.

A few days after painting the main body shell, I took the wraps off the bonnet which I had painted some months previously and discovered that it was a rather different shade from the more recently applied paint. I wet flatted the bonnet with 1000 grit, then gave it just a couple of coats of cellulose from the same batch I had used on the rest of the car. The semi-restoration was over.

The car achieved a first-time MOT pass. I had new headlining fitted by Bernie Lewis, a local trimmer, and was so impressed with his work that I commissioned him to make and fit a new pair of seat covers. For the first time since I bought the car, it is smart, mechanically sorted and – with the fitment of a new steering rack – a complete joy to drive.

And it's not for sale!

CHAPTER FOUR

Surviving Breakdowns

The simplicity of the MGB helps make it an especially reliable car, and many owners have covered vast distances in properly maintained MGBs with not a hint of trouble and without any major repairs becoming necessary. However, all MGBs are now old cars, and like old cars of all types they have a predominance of old components, some of which have many years' life left in them, some of which are nearing the end of their days, and a few of which could turn up their toes at any time. In order to enjoy trouble-free motoring it is necessary to monitor the condition of these components whenever you drive or service the car, and to try to predict which of them might give trouble before they do fail.

Some breakdowns are of course caused by unpredictable mechanical faults, such as broken half shafts, seized gearboxes and broken connecting rods, although the vast majority of roadside breakdowns are probably caused by more avoidable failures of components in the fuel and particularly the ignition system rather than by faults occurring in the engine or drive train. Merely supplementing your regular maintenance routine with a visual inspection of fuel lines (check for corrosion of the metal fuel pipes on older cars) and ignition wiring for cuts and abrasions can help to prevent many breakdowns.

The simple maintenance routines described in the earlier chapter will also go a long way to help avoiding the chances of a mechanical breakdown, but there are extra precautions which will not only help prevent breakdowns but also allow you to deal with them if they do arise.

It is well worth carrying a basic 'get you home' repair kit in the car at all times. The minimum such kit might consist of an adjustable spanner and preferably a set of imperial spanners, a spark plug box spanner, emery cloth, sturdy pliers with a built-in side cutter, and a small selection of screwdrivers. Many suitable motorists' tool kits are available, and they are usually packaged in plastic carrying cases which not only keep the tools together, dry and in one place, but also stop them from rattling as the car is driven! Supplement this with a tow rope, jumper leads, electrical insulation tape, a small selection of wire end terminals, self-tapping screws, fuses, lengths of wire, plus water for the radiator and perhaps a litre of engine oil. And, of course, a foot pump. In many countries you have by law to carry a warning triangle in the car at all times and, legal requirement or not, it is recommended that you keep one in the car boot.

Before you set out on a journey it is well worth taking a few seconds to carry out simple

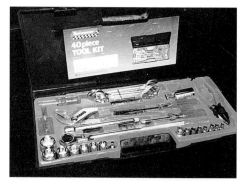

'Get you home' toolkit. Small toolkits like this are available at most motor factors, and can prove invaluable if not life-savers on occasion! Although the individual tools are of indifferent quality, they won't wear out because they are intended to be used infrequently - hopefully never.

checks. Visually check the tyres for inflation, bulges and for any signs of damage. Check that the lights and brake lights work, and that the headlights are as bright as usual (the battery could be running down). When you turn the engine over, note whether it turns as fast as usual and, when it fires up, check the oil pressure gauge immediately and keep an eye on the ignition light to ensure that it goes out, signifying that the battery is indeed being charged. Any new phenomena, such as blue smoke or steam – smoke slowly drifts away, steam disappears – from the exhaust (worn or broken piston rings, worn valve stems/guides allowing oil into cylinders or damaged head gasket/cracked head or block allowing in coolant – all require specialist attention) or unusual sounds when the engine fires up, are warning signs that all is not well, and remedial action should follow as soon as possible. A deep rumbling noise on first starting the engine could possibly be a not too serious fault, or it could – and most probably does – indicate worn main/big end bearings. Seek professional assistance!

Preparing for a long journey is a more serious matter. The tyres (including the spare) should be checked with a gauge for correct inflation and they should be checked thoroughly for tread depth, cuts, abrasions and bulges. Check the tightness of the wheel nuts or spinners.

Lift the bonnet. Check the levels of the fluid in the brake and clutch reservoirs. If either is substantially low then it will pay to have the cause established and dealt with before a long journey is undertaken. If a level is down just a little then top it up. Check the engine oil level and again, if it is unduly low then seek and remedy the cause before undertaking a long journey, but top up if it has dropped just a little since last checked. Check the level in the windscreen washer bottle. Check the coolant level and top up if a little low but investigate if very much coolant is being lost. Examine the fan belt for cuts and general wear (a snapped fan belt is a very common cause of breakdowns – smart people carry a spare) and replace if necessary.

Start the engine, check the oil pressure gauge and ignition warning light, then check all electrical equipment for correct functioning, including the lighting system. It is not a bad idea also to check the battery electrolyte level.

Before setting out on a long journey it is worth obtaining a few spare parts which can often get you out of trouble. These are, a fan belt, a distributor cap and points/condenser, spark plugs and their leads, and light bulbs. It is a good idea also to carry water for the radiator, a litre of oil, a spray can of light oil (for spraying onto the ignition components if they get wet) and a small container of brake/clutch fluid. One final point regarding long journeys. And yes, I know it's a ridiculous one, but it has to be made. Do ensure that you have enough fuel or that there are sufficient petrol stations en route! Many people carry a can of petrol in the boot of their car – I personally prefer not to carry liquid which gives off combustible fumes anywhere other than in the fuel tank.

Those who carry out no work on their cars themselves would do well to have their cars serviced and checked at a service centre immediately before embarking on a long journey. Membership of one of the national breakdown organisations would obviously also be a good precaution.

Those who do carry out even limited home servicing of their MGBs can help avert breakdowns by checking components which might not normally be dealt with during a service. Examining the state of wiring can reveal signs of overheating which, if left unattended, could be the cause of an electrical fire. Examining the state of the fuel tank sides and base, plus the fuel lines could reveal a small leak destined to turn into a substantial one if left to its own devices.

An awareness of the sounds and smells of your car when underway is a priceless aid to predicting looming faults. Any new noise or unfamiliar aroma could turn out to be a symptom of an expensive fault (if not immediately remedied) or the cause of a future breakdown. Any apparent fault should be investigated at the earliest opportunity, and always remember that no mechanical nor electrical fault can ever 'cure' itself – if a suspicious noise suddenly stops, the chances are that far from the fault curing itself, it has entered the next stage of its progress towards complete breakdown.

FLAT TYRE

Most drivers will suffer a punctured tyre at some point in their motoring careers, and those who have never changed a wheel might care to take the precaution of practising doing so in the comfort and safety of their own driveway in preparation for the time they have to do it For Real.

Firstly, although you should never in normal circumstances drive a car which has a flat tyre, do get the car to a place of safety (driving as slowly as possible) before stopping. On the motorway this is the hard shoulder. On ordinary roads, don't drive miles looking for a lay-by, because the tyre will come off the rim and you'll destroy both tyre and wheel; find a straight section of road where other motorists can see you in plenty of time – never stop on a bend in the road. If you have a warning triangle or anything else which will warn drivers to slow down before they reach you, put it out. If your car is fitted with hazard warning lights, switch them on. At night, at the very least leave your side-lights on.

Get the spare wheel out and check that it's inflated properly. Engage the handbrake and place the car in gear. If you can find a couple of stones (or keep chocks in the car) for the front wheel which is to remain on the ground then use them. Slacken the spinners (wire wheel cars – you presumably carry a suitable copper mallet for this purpose in the car at all

times) or nuts, then jack up the offending side of the car, using the reinforced jacking point provided mid-way along the sill underside.

Remove the spinner or nuts, pull the wheel off, offer up the spare and re-fit the spinner or wheel nuts. Tighten these until the wheel is securely held, then lower the car to the ground and remove the jack. The spinners or nuts now have to be finally tightened, and many people don't seem to know how much to tighten either! With wheel nuts, don't overdo it by

Hitting the spinner. To avoid belting and damaging your wheel wires, ensure that the hand which swings to copper/rawhide mallet is in line with the wheel hub, so that the closest the mallet gets to the wheel is at the centre of the swing.

Hub splines. It is worth putting plenty of grease on the hub splines (wire wheels). If you have to change a wheel at the roadside, remove it when you return to the workshop and grease the splines.

jumping up and down on the end of the wheel-brace – remember that you will have to get them off again – firm pressure with your arm muscles will be perfectly sufficient. With spinners, it seems that you can keep on hitting the ears ad infinitum and still they turn a fraction with each clout of the copper mallet! Again, don't overdo it, but tighten them to the point at which a gentler clout in the opposite direction is insufficient to move them. In both cases, it is as well to check the tightness of wheel fixings after having driven the car for a few miles.

AN INTRODUCTION TO FUEL AND ELECTRICS

It is far easier to trace faults in the electrical and fuel delivery systems (the two major causes of roadside breakdowns) if you have a basic understanding of how these work. Of the two, the fuel delivery system is the simpler, so we'll take a look at this first. The following is not a treatise on the workings of the automobile, but considers only specific areas which typically contribute to breakdowns.

Petrol is stored in and drawn from the fuel tank by an electric pump, which pushes it into a fuel bowl in each carburettor. A float within the fuel bowl operates a valve when the bowl becomes full, so cutting off the supply of fuel. The fuel pump automatically stops pumping when this happens.

As the engine turns over, air is drawn into it through the carburettor throat, in which the main jet is situated. There is petrol in the jet, and the effective diameter of the jet is controlled by a tapered needle which can rise and fall in accordance with the amount of air being drawn into the engine. As air rushes through the carburettor throat, its density and hence its pressure drops, and this causes two things to happen. Firstly, a piston (which holds the main jet needle) in the top of the carburettor (the dashpot) rises within the dashpot. This occurs

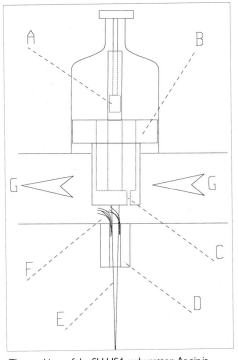

The workings of the SU HS4 carburettor. As air is drawn through the throat (G), its pressure decreases. A slight vacuum extends into the piston chamber (bell housing) above the piston (B) via the connecting port (C), causing the piston to rise. The piston pulls the tapered needle (E) upwards, so increasing the effective surface area of the fuel in the main jet (D), so that more enters the airstream as fine droplets (F). The HIF carburettors fitted to later cars are more complicated than the HS4 of early cars, though the basic principles of operation are the same. The main jet of the HIF carb is held by a bi-metallic bracket, which varies its height and hence the richness of the mixture, according to temperature. To vary the mixture, a screw on the main body acts on the bi-metallic bracket. Choke is provided by a separate jet. A good workshop manual should include details of stripping and servicing the HIF.

because an air passage connects the volume above the piston to the carburettor throat, and the reduction in air pressure in the throat draws air from the dashpot chamber, lowering its pressure and hence drawing the piston upwards. The piston draws the needle upwards with it, which effectively enlarges the opening in the main jet.

The second thing which happens is that the low pressure air rushing through the carburettor throat draws tiny droplets of petrol from the jet, so that a mixture of fine droplets of petrol and air enter the combustion chambers. This mixture is ignited by a sparking plug to provide the energy to power the car.

The choke operates by pulling the main jet downwards (HS4 carburettors), or by bringing another jet into play (HIF carburettors) so that more fuel is drawn into the mixture in relation to the quantity of air, giving a 'rich' mixture to help start the engine on cold mornings.

The fuel system also contains fuel filters, which trap any foreign bodies in the fuel, such as tiny rust flakes from the inside of the fuel tank and any objects which might fall into the fuel tank filler neck when the car is being re-fuelled. We'll come back to the fuel pump after looking at the electricity which powers it.

ELECTRICS

The electrical system is more complicated to explain, and we'll start at the very beginning by looking at what electricity is. You can't touch it, you can't smell or see it – so just what is electricity? Think of a length of copper wire (electricity spends most of its time in copper wires) at the atomic level. Each atom is surrounded by many orbiting electrons, some of which are not held in orbit too strongly by their nucleus. When no electrical current is flowing, some of these electrons become detached from their atoms and fly off to collide with other atoms which, in turn, can have one of their electrons knocked out of orbit. This movement

of electrons is random BUT, when the two ends of the wire are connected to a battery, there exists a glut of electrons at one end and two few at the other, a potential difference which causes electrons to flow through the wire from one terminal to the other – in other words, the random flights of electrons have been replaced with a steady, directional flow.

So electricity can be defined as a controlled flow of electrons, but how is this put to use? In the automotive sense, there are two side-effects of electrical current flow of interest; electricity flowing through a material generates heats and magnetic fields. Heat is generated when the flow reaches an area of resistance – a material whose atoms hold on to their electrons rather more tightly than do conductive materials such as copper, gold and silver. The resistive metals used in light bulbs are the most obvious example; run electricity through them and they get hot – so hot, in fact, that they give out bright light. Were they not surrounded in an inert gas inside the glass bulb which prevents combustion from occurring then they would burn through in a fraction of a second. Other areas of resistance are corroded connections, a length of damaged wire with reduced cross section area or a wire of too-small a cross sectional area – if it allows electricity to pass through but restricts the flow then it will become hot.

While on the subject of wires, the cross sectional area of wire must increase in accordance with the quantity of electricity it will have to handle. A side-light wire carries only a small current and so is of thin section wire while the starter motor wires carry a huge current and so they are very thick. If too much electricity is drawn through too thin a wire, the wire will quickly become hot, and burn off its insulation.

Magnetism is another matter. When current flows through a wire, a weak magnetic field is created around the wire. This is too low in power to be of any automotive use, but if the length of wire is coiled up so that a great length of wire occupies a small space, then the strength of the field is increased and can do a lot of work. We'll look at the coil which generates the charge for the spark plugs later.

For our purposes, we'll consider two utilisations of electro-magnets. The starter solenoid is an electro-magnet which, when power flows through its coil, generates sufficient magnetic force to pull a metal bar which completes another electric circuit, but one which requires very high levels of energy – the starter motor circuit. The first section of the ignition system (from the ignition switch to the starter solenoid coil) carries only small currents, which is important not only because it saves having to run yards of heavy-duty cable but also for safety reasons. You turn on the ignition and the ignition circuit is energised, turn the key a little more and the starter solenoid completes a heavy-duty circuit to turn the starter motor.

The second electro-magnet operated component to consider is the fuel pump. Two simple flaps (non-return valves) allow petrol into and out of a chamber, depending on whether there is suction or pressure. The suction which draws petrol from the tank and the pressure which pushes it towards the carburettors is provided by a diaphragm which moves backwards and forwards to vary the volume of the chamber. The diaphragm is powered by an electromagnet and a spring.

When the carburettor float drops and opens the valve to accept fuel from the pump, the metal core and with it the diaphragm is pushed forwards by a spring, pushing fuel out of the chamber and towards the carburettor. When the diaphragm and metal core are fully forwards, this closes a set of points (electrical contacts) at the rear of the unit, completing a circuit which energises the electro-magnet. This pulls the core, and hence the diaphragm, backwards, sucking petrol into the chamber. When the core is fully back, the points open, the electro-magnet is 'off' and the spring pushes the core and diaphragm forwards,

pushing petrol from the outlet, until the points again close and the process is re-started. When the fuel bowl is full and the inlet is sealed, the pressure in the pump outlet pipe is great enough to stop the spring from pushing forwards. Next time you switch on the ignition first thing in the morning, listen for the clicking noise made by the fuel pump.

Onto the battery. Most people believe that the car battery stores electricity – wrong! The car battery houses metallic and chemical substances which, when a load (a light bulb, wiper or starter motor etc.) is connected, begin a reversible chemical process. Inside the battery are a number of cells each containing two dissimilar metal plates in a weak acid solution

Checking the battery with a multi-meter. This is the 'clean' way to check battery condition – also quicker and easier than measuring the Specific Gravity in all of the cells using a hydrometer.

(electrolyte). When you throw a switch and complete the circuit between the two terminals, electrons flow from one type of plate to the other, changing the chemical composition of each and in the process generating a small electrical current of just over two volts. A six volt battery contains three cells, a twelve volt battery contains six.

The chemical process in a car battery is reversible; that is, when the generator (dynamo or alternator) creates an electrical current, some is fed to the battery and reverses the process so that the two metals return to their former composition, 're-charging' the battery.

To save on wiring, the chassis (body) of the car, being composed of metal which conducts electricity, is substituted for one of the wires needed to complete a circuit. The body in this respect is known as the 'earth' (UK) or 'ground' (USA). So, a wire runs from a terminal, through a switch to a device – a light bulb or whatever – through the device, into the bodyshell and back to the other terminal, which is connected to the body by the earth strap. While on the subject of earths, electric currents in a circuit actively seek these out because they are the channel of least resistance back to the battery – if a wire leading to a light bulb, for instance, shorts to earth, then the current will take this easier route rather than pass through the light bulb, in the process, drawing excessive current and blowing a fuse or damaging the wiring.

We've looked at electricity, wires and batteries; what next? The ignition system (which causes more breakdowns than anything else).

When you operate the ignition key, the ignition circuit energises a coil of wire called the primary winding within the body of the ignition coil. Also within the coil is a secondary winding called – wait for it – the secondary winding, which has many times more individual coils than the primary winding. A strong magnetic field builds up around the primary winding and, when the circuit which feeds it is

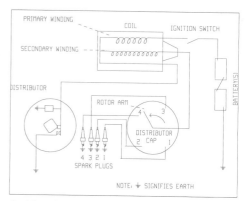

Ignition circuit. A simplified diagram of the ignition circuit. The points are shown open, when the capacitor (above the points and cam within the distributor) comes into play. See text.

Inside the coil. These are the primary and secondary windings, along with their core. You will note that the windings are concentric – they are not shown as such in wiring diagrams.

broken, the magnetic field collapses and induces an electrical charge in the secondary winding. Because the secondary winding has many times more coils than the primary, the voltage created is much higher – 25,000 volts – which is sufficiently high to be able to jump across small gaps to find an earth. Both windings are cooled by oil contained within the coil casing. The coil can overheat – incidentally – and its case split if the ignition is left switched on for long periods with the points closed and the engine not running. So far so good.

Inside the distributor, the points are closed and it is these which complete the circuit to earth which energises the primary winding in the coil. As the engine turns over, one of the distributor drive shaft cam lobes opens the points, so breaking that circuit, so that the magnetic field of the primary winding breaks down, generating the high voltage in the secondary winding, which immediately looks for an earth, escaping into the main coil to the distributor High Tension lead. The primary circuit may have been broken by the points opening, but the residual electric charge in the primary coil is quite strong enough to jump across the points to find an earth. As you will remember, areas of resistance generate heat, and the air gap in the points is one such area.

Because having electricity jump across the points between two thousand and ten thousand times a minute (at engine revolutions of 1,000 rpm and 5,000 rpm respectively) would rapidly burn away the points, the distributor is fitted with a condenser. This contains two rolled-up sheets of conductive metal, separated by an insulator, so that the two cannot touch. The residual electric charge in the primary coil doesn't know this, and rushes into the condenser thinking that it is an earth instead of jumping the gap between the points, so saving the points. Once the charge gets into the condenser, it realises it's been duped (pretty dumb, these electrical charges) and, because the points will by then have closed again to complete the circuit, it turns around and heads back for the primary winding and helps energise it ready for the next time that the points open.

At the very same time, the rotor arm in the distributor is whizzing round and round, past the terminals in the distributor cap to which the sparking plug high tension leads are connected. It is adjacent to each terminal as the points are opening and the 25,000 volts are headed up the main high tension lead for the charge to sense a path to earth. The high tension lead from the coil tower (along which the charge from the winding is running) leads via the centre of the distributor cap and a carbon contact to the metal strip on the top of the rotor arm, and the charge jumps across into the sparking plug high tension lead terminal and heads off in the direction of the spark plug, trying to find an earth to complete the circuit. When it gets there, it finds that it has to jump yet another gap (the spark plug gap) to get to earth, in so doing, providing the spark to ignite the fuel/air mixture within the cylinder. Pretty straightforward?

ENGINE REFUSES TO TURN OVER

The least traumatic place to suffer a breakdown is on the drive at home, and happily, this is where the majority of breakdowns reportedly occur. Carry out the simplest checks first and leave the fancy stuff till later.

If the ignition light dims as the key is turned but no noise emanates from the starter motor, then check the battery connections. A loose or corroded connection can in some instances supply enough power for, say, the lights, but not enough for the starter motor. Also check the earth strap/bodywork connection for tightness and corrosion.

If the connections are good, the chances are that the battery is run down, meaning either that it is in poor condition and unable to hold a charge, that you left the lights switched on overnight or that the generator is not delivering a full charge. You can check whether the battery is nearly flat by switching on the headlights and adjudging their brightness. Check the electrolyte level; if it is substantially down then the generator is probably over-charging the battery – in the case of a dynamo, the regulator needs attention, alternators should be exchanged.

Tapping starter solenoid. A sticking starter solenoid can sometimes be freed by giving the body a sharp clout – don't use a hammer; the handle of a medium-sized screwdriver should suffice.

Whilst you can bump start the car or use jumper leads to get a car with a flat battery going, you should not travel anywhere other than to a place of repair unless you possess a multi meter and are able to check that the battery is being charged.

If the battery seems OK, check the connections to the starter solenoid and the starter motor. Have an assistant operate the ignition switch whilst you listen for the starter solenoid 'click'. The solenoid, as we have already established, is an electrically operated switch which carries the huge current needed by the starter motor and which is activated by a very small current from the ignition switch. If it isn't operating, try giving it a sharp tap with a spanner or similar (car out of gear – keep clear of moving parts), and try again.

If the solenoid is operating (you can hear it click), then the starter motor may be jammed – more common with inertia starters. If so, place the car in fourth gear (ignition OFF), disengage the handbrake and rock the car forwards and backwards, which can often free a jammed starter. Alternatively, give the body of the motor a clout with a mallet. If the engine still won't turn over, you'll have to replace the sole-

noid or replace/repair the starter motor as appropriate – either way, you ain't going anywhere. The problem could be cured with new starter motor brushes or pinion, or in the worst scenario it could necessitate replacement of the flywheel ring gear, so seek professional advice.

ENGINE TURNS OVER BUT WON'T FIRE

Don't just sit there churning the engine over – all you'll accomplish by this is running the battery flat.

CLEAN HANDS Is there fuel in the tank? Could the fuel pump (mounted on the outer heelboard) be heard to click when the ignition switch was firstly turned on? (faulty pump). Is there an aroma of petrol from the exhaust tail pipe just after the engine has been turned over? – if so, fuel is reaching the engine and the fault probably lies with the ignition. Turn the ignition switch off and raise the bonnet. You're going to have to get your hands dirty.

IGNITION Check the connections at either end of the main HT lead running from the coil to the distributor cap. Check the other wires attached to the coil, and remake any poor connections. Check the high tension leads and distributor cap – if these have moisture on them then dry them off because they are allowing the charge which should go to the spark plugs to go to earth instead – and spray or preferably use a cloth to wipe on a thin coating of light oil and then try again to start the car.

If the engine still refuses to fire, switch off the ignition, pull the main HT feed from the distributor cap and hold this gently (if you possess the proper insulated pliers for the job – otherwise, try to tape it into position) a fraction of an inch from a good earth, well away from the fuel supply and the spark plug holes. Get an assistant to turn the engine over for a couple of seconds and observe whether a spark can be seen to

If the engine turns but refuses to fire, you can quickly check that the ignition circuit is energised by opening the points (ignition switched on). There will be a 'splash' across the points – if not, use a tester (a light bulb with leads will do) to re-check.

Drying the plug leads. Always keep a few pieces of cloth in the car – you never know when you might have to dry the plug leads – driving through a rainstorm or a puddle can be sufficient to knock out the ignition.

Temperature variations can mean lots of condensation – moisture appearing out of thin air on any cold surfaces. What you see on the wing here will be repeated under the bonnet, and the distributor cap and all HT leads will most probably also be wet. Dry them and spray on moisture repellant.

Distributor cap. The tiniest crack in the distributor cap can hold moisture, which will cause non-starting problems. Replace damaged caps.

jump between the HT lead and the earth – accompanied by an audible clicking sound. If not then either the coil or its feed is probably the cause. If there is a spark, then (ignition switch off) replace the HT lead in the distributor cap, remove the distributor cap and inspect it minutely for cracks which could contain moisture. Also check for signs of arcing – rough-edged black lines which contain carbon which forms a highly conductive path for electricity and channels it away from the correct spark plug. A temporary repair can be effected by scratching out the carbon, but the distributor cap should be replaced. Check that the points open and close freely and that their contacts are clean and not heavily pitted. If the points are

HT lead/plug taped to earth. Don't hold the HT lead in your hand or it will belt you! If you don't have insulated spark plug pliers to hand, tape the plug to earth well away from the spark plug holes.

Checking the fuel delivery. Be cautious when attempting this test – the ignition should be switched on for no more than a couple of seconds, and you must ensure that all of the fuel which is pumped is safely caught in a container of some sort.

dirty, clean them and try to start the engine.

When starting a car using the choke, more than at any other time, the rich fuel/air mixture in the cylinders needs a good, strong spark from the plugs. Loose plug end fittings cause a loss of electrical energy to the sparking plugs and hence a weak spark, so check that the end fittings are all tight. If these are found to be loose, remove the spark plugs and dry off their ends – they will be covered with petrol.

Remove and check the spark plugs visually for obvious damage such as cracked ceramics, for heavy carbon deposits (wire brush this off, and make a note to have the carburation set – the engine is running too rich), sticky black deposits (clean off but make note to investigate at the first opportunity why oil is finding its way into the cylinders – could be broken or worn piston rings, valve stem to valve guide clearance), glazing (engine running far too hot – get professional advice and don't run the engine in this state), and correct gap (adjust). Then place each plug in turn in its lead and tape it to a good earth away from the fuel deliv-

ery system, carburettors and plug holes (or hold it using the proper insulated pliers) and have the engine turned over to see whether there is a spark. Absence of a spark could be due to a faulty plug or lead, so try apparently faulty plugs on other leads to establish which is at fault: replace any faulty plugs or leads.

FUEL Fuel delivery problems are far less common causes of non-starting engines than ignition faults. Pull the main fuel line from the forward carburettor (it is as well to wrap a cloth around the pipe end before removing it because if the pump is working then there will be residual pressure in the system) and place the end in a jar or similar container while an assistant turns the ignition switch on (so that the ignition light comes on – there is no need to spin the engine) for a second or two. If fuel pumps from the line, then replace it on the carburettor. If no fuel is forthcoming, check the in-line fuel filter (where fitted, generally to later cars – although a blocked filter should have been apparent as a developing fault – lumpy

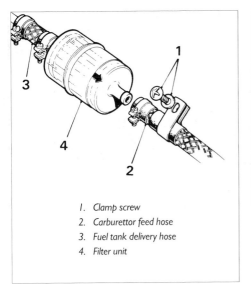

1. Clamp screw
2. Carburettor feed hose
3. Fuel tank delivery hose
4. Filter unit

Fuel filter. Replace the in-line fuel filter (where fitted) annually or if a partial blockage is suspected. Do make sure that you fit it the correct way around – the arrow in the body indicates the direction of fuel flow. (Courtesy Autodata.)

Tapping the fuel pump body. A sticking fuel pump can sometimes be started by giving the body a sharp tap. This is only a 'get you home' measure – replace the pump at the earliest opportunity – the next time it fails you could be when you're in the fast lane of a motorway!

The filter in situ on a 1979 MGB. It is as well to place a rag underneath the filter before disconnecting the feed pipe – just in case it is blocked and there is pressure in the fuel in the pump to filter hose.

running, intermittent loss of power – for some time) and suspect a faulty pump. A sharp tap on the pump body can sometimes rectify sticking points, although it is recommended that the pump is attended to at the earliest opportunity before it lets you down again.

If fuel is available but the engine still won't start, then it could be flooded, which should have been apparent when you inspected the (wet, smelling strongly of petrol) spark plugs. The engine can flood because either the choke jams or too much choke has been applied for the conditions, because the carburettor float(s) jam or most commonly the inlet needle is held in the open position by dirt. It is easy to check that the choke operates correctly. To clear dirt from the inlet valve, pinch the fuel line with the engine turning over so that the float chamber fuel level drops – then release the line and the gush of fuel through the inlet valve will normally do the trick. If this fails, the float could be mal-adjusted (not all are adjustable) or leaking (it sinks).

Carburettor overflow pipe. If fuel gushes out of the overflow pipe DON'T use the car until the sticking float or defective needle and valve have been attended to.

In such cases, fuel should spill from the carburettor overflow pipe(s) rather than flood the engine. The engine will flood if the ends of these are blocked because this causes back-pressure which prevents the floats from rising and closing the inlet valve. The overflow pipe lower ends are situated just over a lip in the engine block casting, and most commonly block if they are taken off and re-fitted and accidentally pushed into the mixture of oil and much which lives on this ledge. Check the pipes, if they're not blocked then consult a workshop manual or send for the cavalry!

STARTER MOTOR WORKS BUT DOES NOT TURN ENGINE

With inertia starters, check the condition of the battery – a flat battery cannot spin the motor quickly enough to engage the drive mechanism. Check that the starter motor mounting bolts are holding it securely and, if so, the problem is probably a sticking pinion or a broken drive spring. You could bump start the car, but what if you stall it at the lights? Best to forget using the car until the problem has been rectified.

If fuel doesn't gush out of the overflow pipe(s), the engine could still be flooding – the symptoms include very high fuel consumption, sometimes accompanied by backfiring.

ENGINE STARTS, BUT RUNS LUMPILY AND BACKFIRES WHEN REVVED

This is not a common fault, but can occur when one or more spark plugs or leads are duff. Unburnt fuel mixture from the affected cylinder(s) passes into the exhaust manifold, where it can be ignited by hot or still-burning gasses from other cylinders which causes it to explode, and hence the backfiring.

Check each plug and lead in turn as already described for a spark.

ENGINE WANTS TO FIRE BUT WON'T RUN

This is normally a sign of fuel starvation, caused by a blocked fuel filter, non-functioning choke on cold mornings or air induction. Check the fuel delivery as already described, check that the choke cable pulls the jets down (HS4 carburettor) and check the vacuum advance pipe and (where fitted) overdrive vacuum switch pipe connections on the inlet manifold.

Later cars are fitted with a six volt coil with an internal ballast resistor. The ballast resistor offers little resistance when it is cold but this rises as it becomes warm, so that you get a good strong spark for cold starts but less when the engine has warmed.

A malfunctioning ballast resistor can give a weak spark when you most need it and prevent the engine from starting: it can also (as has happened to the author) be responsible for a disconnection in the ignition circuit, so try replacing the coil.

ENGINE 'HUNTS'

If one carburettor is faulty (blocked jet, sticking float, piston/bell housing wear) then the engine will run hesitantly, because some cylinders receive a very weak mixture and others a normal mix. Seek professional help or consult a workshop manual.

TICKS OVER POORLY ON THREE CYLINDERS; ALL FOUR FIRE WHEN REVVED

This is normally caused by a break in a copper cored plug lead. A breakage can occur which is temporarily 'welded' as the engine revs but breaks again on tickover when engine movement is more exaggerated. Disconnect each lead in turn until the faulty one is found.

UNRELIABLE STARTERS/ 'PROBLEM' CARS

Some cars seem never able to be relied upon to start first time every time. Some won't start with the engine cold; others with the engine hot. Some cars never seem to give their best and can appear un-tuneable. In either case, give the car a major service, which entails replacing most ignition components and setting up the timing and carburation correctly (the carburation is best set by professionals; all UK MOT testing stations now have exhaust gas analysers with which they can get it spot on, so why try yourself without such a handy and infallible device?).

Also, replace any filters in the fuel delivery system and check the fuel pump points for corrosion which could cause intermittent fuel delivery problems. If this fails to cure the problems, exchange the fuel pump.

If you don't feel able to do this then have the car serviced by an MGB specialist. It is worth having the cylinder compression checked (this only takes a few minutes and won't cost too much) or buying a meter and testing it yourself. The compression should be 160 psi for high compression ratio B series engines, or 130 psi with low compression engines. If one or more cylinders are substantially down, then squirt a little engine oil through the spark plug hole and re-test. The oil will temporarily improve the piston ring seal and, if the compression rises with the oil, the fault is connected with the piston rings and/or worn cylinder bores (a re-

125

This is how to strip an H54 carburettor. Removing the dashpot reveals the piston.

Lifting the needle/piston. Take care not to bend the needle when lifting the piston, and don't leave the assembly where it could get damaged.

Removing the fuel bowl top. Fuel flooding is sometimes caused by no more than a speck of dirt between the needle and jet. Try pinching the fuel delivery line while the engine is running, then releasing it. The resultant gush of fuel can clean out such dirt. To get at the float and needle/valve, remove the float chamber top. Never do this, of course, with the ignition switched on – fuel would flood out.

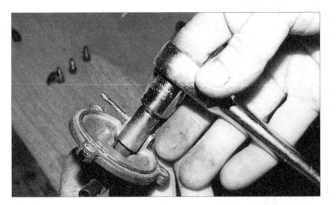

Use a $^{11}/_{32}$" socket or spanner to undo the jet.

The needle simply lifts out. Look for a wear ridge and replace the needle and jet as a set if defective or worn.

Removing the main jet. To remove the main jet, detach the fuel pipe, which is held by a single philips head screw.

The jet can now be pulled out of its bearing.

Butterfly spindle. You can strip the butterfly spindle and remove it from the carburettor body for reaming and bushing, but it is recommended that you have the whole carburettor reconditioned professional

Fuel pump points. The fuel pump points don't usually corrode if the car is in regular use; following a period of inactivity, the points may need cleaning. The text books tell you not to use emery for this; I did six years ago and have had no problems with the unit since!

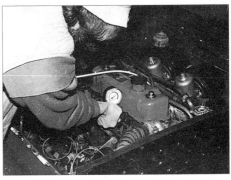

Checking the cylinder compression. Checking the cylinder compression can reveal problems with poor sealing due to worn bores, worn or damaged piston rings, worn or damaged valves and seats. Plugs out, HT leads and distributor cap removed from engine bay.

This can be a one-man operation. Simply operate the starter solenoid manually to spin the engine. The readings from all four cylinders must be fairly close to each other.

bore and oversize pistons are needed) – if there is no change then the valves are the culprit and a cylinder head overhaul is required.

Provided that a B series engine is reasonable condition – the cylinder head is not carboned or cracked, the head gasket is intact and the valves and their seats not damaged (all of which will be revealed during a simple de-coke) – fundamental problems with major fuel or ignition components are the most likely cause of unreliable starting, intermittent performance/high fuel consumption, pinking and other long-term problems.

Given that the engine (which, if suspect, can be swapped for an exchange reconditioned unit) is in good condition and that no apparent faults lie in the ignition or fuel delivery systems, many long-term problems can be cured by exchanging the distributor or the carburettors for reconditioned units. Typical faults include air induction through the carburettor throttle spindle bushes (which, on a reconditioned carburettor, will have been reamed out and re-bushed) and wear in the distributor. A rough and ready check for air induction via the throttle spindle is to spray a little carburettor

Spraying the carb cleaner onto the throttle spindle. Air induction via the throttle spindle means that although the mixture may be adjusted to the correct richness at tickover, when the revs rise the proportion of neat air being drawn in via the leak will vary, and the mixture will be out. With the engine ticking over, spray a little carburettor cleaner onto the ends of the spindles; if the revolutions increase, you have induction, and the spindle holes require reaming and bushing.

Measuring voltage drop across points. A weak spark will have an adverse affect on performance and fuel economy, as well as causing cold starting problems. If voltage drop is more than a third of a volt, clean the points and re-check. If the drop is still excessive, renew the points.

cleaner, WD40 or even engine oil onto the spindle ends. This temporarily seals them (if they are leaking) and if the engine now runs at higher tickover revolutions then you have traced the cause of the problem.

Distributor wear can be traced by checking the dwell angle with a good automotive multi-meter (the dwell angle is the percentage or angle of the distributor shaft rotation during which the points are closed, when the coil primary winding is charging) – a fluctuating dwell angle reading indicates wear in the distributor shaft bearings and results in equal variations in ignition timing. Too small a dwell angle gives a weak spark.

If you possess an automotive multi-meter then there is very little in the ignition system which you cannot test to find faults. Probably the most frequently used scale is the resistance reading (ohms) which allows you to locate disconnections (open circuits), test the coil windings and various connections. Working as a voltmeter, a multi-meter can be used to measure voltage drop across components and connections. Perhaps more importantly, it can measure voltage drop across the points when

connected to the low tension lead and a good earth – anything more than 0.3V is unacceptable and usually indicates resistance across the points or occasionally between the base plate and the distributor body. Automotive multi-meters don't cost too much, and are well worth investing in. The author uses a Gunson Test Tune which, in addition to tracing simple open circuits (disconnections) can be used to test battery condition and charging, dwell angle, voltage drop and earth leakage. Costing less than a full professional service, such meters are highly recommended.

Air induction can be difficult to pin down because the air could – assuming all fastenings are tight – be entering via a damaged inlet manifold gasket, the overdrive vacuum switch pipe or just one carburettor via the throttle spindle or the vacuum advance pipe. The usual symptom of air induction is lumpy tickover. Obviously, a portable exhaust gas tester will allow you to discover any such symptoms, although a throttle spindle leak can be proven by putting a little oil on the spindle ends as already described which – if there is induction – will make the mixture richer.

ON-ROAD BREAKDOWNS

The first rule of dealing with breakdowns on the road is not to panic, but to ensure that the car is parked in a safe place. In the case of a motorway this means the hard shoulder, and for safety's sake it is best to get any passengers out of the car and up the embankment. On ordinary roads as well as motorways, set out a warning triangle to advertise the presence of your car in plenty of time for following drivers, especially if you are unable to get the car fully off the road.

Once you are satisfied that everything is safe, investigate the fault. Unless the fault can be traced and rectified quickly, it is advisable to try to summon assistance at the earliest opportunity. You can waste hours fruitlessly

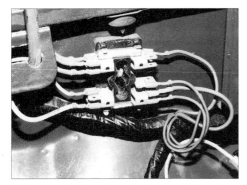

Main fuses. The fuse block of early cars. A blown fuse is not a fault – it is a symptom of a fault which has overloaded the circuit associated with the fuse. Find and rectify that fault before using the car and NEVER replace a blown fuse with one of a higher rating.

looking for fuel or ignition faults (the most common causes of breakdowns), only to eventually discover that a component has totally failed and that repair is impossible without replacement.

A breakdown can become an emergency if, for instance, you continue to drive while ignoring the signs of an electrical fire starting, or if the car should come to a halt on a narrow road in thick fog. Again, don't panic, but try to move the car to a safer position, set out a warning triangle for other road users and get any passengers out of harm's way.

ENGINE 'DIES' OR LOSES POWER

The most common breakdown is when the engine dies or slowly loses power, and – terminal engine problems excepted – this will be due to a fault with either the ignition or the fuel delivery system. Before trying to trace the fault, examine the ignition wiring and the fuel system under the bonnet for danger signs, such as smoke from burning wire insulation or neat

fuel which may have escaped from a fuel line or carburettor. If there is a strong smell of petrol under the bonnet, inside the car or underneath the car then clear passengers and bystanders from the vicinity and summon assistance. If all appears safe, then begin to trace the fault.

If you have just driven through a heavy rain storm, puddle or ford then check first for damp which allows the charge in the high tension leads to earth itself. If the high tension leads or their caps, the distributor or any other part of the ignition system is wet then simply dry it off with a clean cloth, spray on a little water repellant oil if you carry it in the car and try to start the engine.

In dry conditions, if the engine died suddenly without any warning signs then the fault (if electrical) obviously affect all four plugs at once – look firstly for a disconnection within the ignition circuit, starting at the distributor to HT lead and moving back through the system. If the engine misfired before losing power or stopping then start by checking the spark plug caps, then move backwards through the ignition circuit. Bear in mind that ignition faults are most probably the single greatest cause of breakdowns, and check this out first.

If no ignition fault can be traced, then the problem may lie with the fuel delivery. The carburettors are in relative close proximity to the hot exhaust manifold and down pipes, and you should always let these cool before doing anything to the carburettors or fuel lines. There is a strong argument at this stage for calling in assistance, if you have not already done so. Clear any passengers from the car, and quickly check for leakage in the fuel lines.

Fuel delivery problems usually mean that either no fuel is being delivered to the carburettors or that too much fuel is being taken in by the carburettors. The former fault usually lies with the fuel pump, or a blocked filter (or most commonly an empty fuel tank!) and the latter with a sticking float. A sticking float will be apparent from the large amount of fuel which is pumped out of the carburettor overflow pipe(s) when the ignition is turned on (have an assistant turn on the ignition for a second or two whilst you watch for fuel loss) and a fuel pump fault can be confirmed if you switch on the ignition for at most two seconds and listen for the gentle clicking noise which it makes when operating. Unless you know what you are doing, call for assistance.

ENGINE LOSES POWER AND STOPS

Unless you have run out of fuel (in which case the engine would have been coughing and spluttering for a short time before it stopped) then you could have a disconnection or component failure in the ignition system (check as for engine which won't start) or, alternatively, fuel flow might be intermittent. The causes of this can be a blocked fuel tank breather (remove the filler cap and listen for a rush of air into the filler neck) a dirty fuel filter or fuel pump problems.

The engine could be overheating, in which case the coolant temperature gauge should have forewarned you of the problem. Let the engine cool before checking the coolant level.

ENGINE STOPS WITHOUT WARNING

This is almost invariably caused by an ignition fault. Check this as already described.

BREAKDOWN SERVICES

Some breakdown causes cannot be fixed at the roadside, and if you are unable to quickly establish the fault then it is advisable to summon assistance at the earliest opportunity. I reported a non-starting car (NOT my MGB) to one breakdown company at around 9.00 am one day when I was away from home and did not

have access to the necessary tools to trace the fault myself. The breakdown service concerned relied on local garages to respond to any calls. The one-man-band they contacted in my case (a Sunday) was out playing golf, and eventually arrived at 6.00 pm – nine hours after the fault was reported!

My advice is to enrol in a service which is recommended by one of the main MG clubs because, if you are let down by such a company, then you can report the incident to the club and usually obtain some form of redress. Don't rely on back-street operations, but always choose a reputable, nation-wide operation.

Always opt for a service which offers special memberships for classic car owners, because many operations won't cover, for instance, cars over ten years of age. Buy the best you can.

DEVELOPING PROBLEMS

Many problems develop slowly and even those faults which have serious consequences will often only be apparent from their symptoms, their side-effects. For instance, a partially blocked fuel filter can make the mixture too lean and, in time, this can wreck the engine unless rectified. The symptom which will be most apparent is engine overheating. The same symptom, however, can equally signal too-advanced ignition timing, a loose fan belt, coolant loss, blocked radiator and a host of other faults.

When a symptom such as overheating becomes apparent, its cause should be traced and rectified as soon a possible.

Not every developing fault encountered on a journey will necessarily lead to a breakdown before the destination is reached, although there are several problems which can arise which should be investigated the moment it is safe to stop the car. Such faults include a sudden drop in oil pressure, an unexplained rise in coolant temperature or any apparent electrical fault, whether constant or intermittent. All of

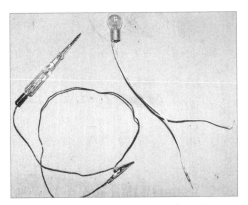

Simple testers. A low cost commercially made tester (left) with its DIY equivalent – a light bulb with two wires soldered on. Earth the lead, and if you touch the other lead (or the probe) against an energised connector or exposed wire the bulb lights. The probe is intended to be pushed through a wire's insulation – not too clever an idea because moisture which subsequently gets into the hole can cause problems.

The tester in use trying to trace a disconnection, starting at the fuse block.

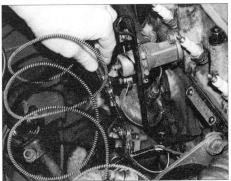

Testing the solenoid. If all electrical systems appear dead, test the starter solenoid, which is fed directly from the battery.

Testing to ascertain whether the ignition system is energised.

these faults can lead in a very short space of time to serious (and invariably expensive) problems. A drop in oil pressure might allow the engine to run long enough to get you to your destination, but you could wreck the engine in the process. A rise in coolant temperature is not a fault in itself but a symptom of a serious fault which could cause extensive engine damage if left unattended. An electrical fault could start an electrical fire at any time, so take these very seriously indeed. Any unusual noises warrant investigation at the earliest opportunity. In addition to engine noises such as knocking or pinking, listen for new noises from the transmission or suspension, and for suddenly excessive road/tyre noise (which may be accompanied by steering wheel vibration – which also warrants investigation).

Pinking (a harmless-sounding tinkling noise which is usually heard with the engine under load) could be caused by air induction and hence a weak mixture, by too-advanced ignition, engine overheating (non-functioning thermostat or faulty water pump) or by several other faults – the noise is made by the pistons as they tip in the bore because the mixture is being ignited too early – the long-term consequences are very expensive, so get it seen to at the earliest opportunity.

Sometimes, these warning signs lead to problems which can be dealt with there and then, sometimes, it is up to the driver to decide whether to carry on and risk damage to the car or whether to summon assistance. Of the faults which can be dealt with, if the engine is pinking, look firstly for an induction air leak. If an irregular knocking noise can be heard, check the tightness of exhaust, suspension and other fittings. If tyre noise can be heard or if vibration is suddenly felt through the steering wheel, check the tyres for bulges or other damage, and fit the spare to the appropriate corner.

SURVIVING ROADWORKS AND QUEUES

Why are roadworks always accompanied by signs which state that such and such an authority apologises for any delay caused when we all know perfectly well that roadworks are sited and timed to cause maximum delays to the greatest number of drivers? To make matters worse, and on a personal note, they always choose the hottest days of the year to resurface roads on which I want to drive – risking an overheated engine in the slow moving queue of traffic caused by said resurfacing. I strongly suspect a conspiracy.

Like many cars, the MGB was built in a period when traffic was much lighter, when roadworks seemed more infrequent and when the only queue of any real substance you'd find on a blisteringly hot bank holiday in the UK was on the then infamous Exeter bypass. Like many cars, MGBs are intended to take advantage of a steady flow of air through the radiator and around the engine to help with the cooling and, if you leave them stationary with the engine running on a hot day for any period of time the temperature gauge will begin to creep in the wrong direction.

An overheated engine can blow its core plugs (all coolant lost and engine wrecked if not immediately turned off), it can boil its coolant and blow the radiator cap off or the radiator up (same results). Even nastier things can happen, but I'm sure you get the general idea that your engine must keep its cool.

Mild overheating can be counteracted by turning the heater and blower up full – not too much of a hardship in a Roadster but hell in a GT unless it's fitted with a full length sunroof. More serious overheating demands that the engine is stopped. This can cause a temporary traffic jam, but the alternative is to let the engine coolant boil and cause a more permanent jam. Pull off the road anywhere safe, turn off the engine and raise the bonnet. DON'T move the radiator cap unless you enjoy getting third-degree scalds.

The worst place to have an overheating engine is in a queue on a motorway when the hard shoulder has been pressed into service as an extra lane. There is simply nowhere to go, and you have the choice of risking a real breakdown and causing a temporary one by switching off the ignition.

If you anticipate being caught up in heavy traffic during the summer, you could consider fitting a lower temperature thermostat to help alleviate overheating. Always ensure that the coolant level is OK and that the fan belt is in excellent condition and correctly tensioned before setting out on a long journey and, if your car is fitted with an electric fan then make sure it's working before leaving home.

SURVIVING IN TOWNS

For some reason, nice paintwork and especially soft tops on unattended sports cars incite a certain class of cretin to perform acts of vandalism. You can't take a slashed soft top (or tonneau, which seems to have the same effect as a soft top) to be invisibly mended at the High Street dry cleaners like a jacket, and so, unpalatable as it may be, a hard top is recommended for Roadsters when in town.

Where you park your car in a town can have a bearing on its well-being: parking in the street is not recommended, and large surface car parks aren't much better. Small attended car parks are always more expensive, but it's worth paying the extra for peace of mind. Alternatively, the author has discovered that large stores just removed from the town centres attract very few vandals and, if you can get away with it, are pretty safe places to park. Leave a receipt from the store in question on the dash top, where it can be seen by patrolling staff looking for non-patrons' cars, and don't blame me if you get privately clamped (always a painful business).

The driving standards of town traffic can be so poor that the owner of a chrome bumper car could well wish he or she had a rubber bumper version to join in the general game of dodgems! The car even isn't safe when parked, and it seems probable that more dents nowadays occur in car parks than on the road. All in all, the author keeps an old Volvo 340 exclusively for his occasional and unavoidable trips into town. It's built like a tank, can give as good as it gets in a smack, and if someone does run into it then it's not the End Of The World.

TROUBLE SHOOTING

The following notes omit one potential cause of every one of the problems listed – major mechanical failure. Remember – if a fault cannot be traced quickly, it is best to summon assistance rather than waste time looking for a problem which you might not be able to deal with at the roadside.

ENGINE REFUSES TO START FROM COLD ENGINE WON'T TURN OVER
Loose/corroded battery connections
Engine earth strap fixings loose
Battery flat – low electrolyte level
Starter connections loose
Solenoid faulty/loose connections
Starter jammed

ENGINE TURNS OVER BUT WON'T FIRE
Fuel tank empty
Fuel pump faulty
HT lead connections poor
Coil connections poor
HT leads/distributor cap wet
HT leads faulty
Distributor cap cracked/arcing
Contact breaker points dirty/seized
Spark plug end fittings loose
Spark plugs damaged/carbonned/oiled/wet
Spark plugs faulty/gap incorrect
Fuel pump defective/filter blocked
Engine flooded
Choke jammed on
Dirt in fuel bowl jet
Carburettor float seized
Fuel overflow pipe(s) blocked

STARTER MOTOR SPINS BUT WON'T TURN ENGINE
Inertia starter – low battery charge – broken drive spring
Inertia and pre-engaged starter motors – starter motor bolts loose
Pinion sticking

Engine Starts, but runs Lumpily and Backfires when Revved
Spark plug/HT lead faulty

Engine wants to Fire but won't Run
Blocked air filters
Non-functioning choke
Air induction via vacuum pipes on inlet
manifold
Faulty coil ballast resistor (later cars)

Engine 'Hunts'
Weak mixture from one carburettor

Engine Ticks Over Poorly on Three Cylinders but all Four Fire When Revved
Breakage in copper-cored HT lead

On-road Breakdowns
Engine Misfires or Loses Power
Fuel tank empty
Fuel filler cap breather blocked
Ignition components wet
Ignition open circuit
Faulty fuel pump
Blocked fuel filter
Sticking carburettor float

Engine Loses Power and Stops
Blocked fuel tank cap breather
Blocked fuel filter
Faulty fuel pump
Engine overheating

Engine Stops Without Warning
Ignition component failure
Developing Problems
Engine Oil Pressure Falls
Oil level low due to loss
Engine overheating
Long-term – worn mains bearings – faulty
oil pump – blocked oil pick-up strainer/filter
– defective oil pressure relief valve

Engine Overheats
Broken/slack fan belt
Faulty electrical cooling fan
Coolant leakage/internal blockage
Thermostat faulty
Engine oil level low
Brakes binding
Weak fuel mixture
Ignition timing fault

Engine Backfires on Overrun
Exhaust system leakage/burnt exhaust
valve(s)

'GET-YOU-HOME' TIPS

The following comprises advised courses of action which may enable you to effect temporary repairs; the advice must be used only in cases where it does not contravene prevailing national or local laws, and the author and publisher can assume no responsibility if advice does conflict with prevailing law.

In the U.K., it is an offence to drive an 'unsafe' car on the public highway and, in fact, some Police Officers are being specially trained to detect any of 200 possible faults which render a car unsafe – they are empowered to prohibit the use of the car there and then. Serious problems which make a car unsafe to drive – including brake failure, lighting failure, almost any electrical, suspension or hydraulic problem – MUST be rectified before the car is driven.

Many developing faults give 'early warning' symptoms which the experienced driver can often recognise, which gives you the opportunity to head straight for the nearest repair workshop or to stop the car before the fault develops further.

When you are driving the car...
WATCH
1. the engine coolant temperature gauge.
2. the oil pressure gauge.
3. the ignition warning light

IF
1. temperature rises.
2. oil pressure falls.
3. ignition light comes on (commonly broken fan/generator drive belt).
THEN
Stop the engine as soon as is consistent with safety and investigate.

DEALING WITH ON-ROAD FAULTS

BROKEN FAN BELT. The 'fan' or more properly generator drive belt is driven by the crankshaft pulley and drives the water pump, engine cooling fan and dynamo on early cars, the water pump and alternator on later cars. The usual first symptom of the broken belt is that the ignition light illuminates, signifying that the battery is no longer being charged.

A car with a broken belt can be driven gently for a very short distance but, on early cars, the lack of cooling effect from the fan coupled with (both early and late cars) a lack of coolant circulation will quickly overheat the engine, and can result in internal engine damage. A battery in good condition will be able to power the ignition circuit for some time, although use of the lights, wiper motor, heater fan and especially the starter motor will reduce this greatly.

It is best to drive the car only to a known nearby place of safety or repair – don't drive away in the hope of finding something – the car could break down and leave you stranded in an even worse place.

Temporary fan belts are available, although those setting out on a long journey would do better to pack a spare belt, plus spanners and a lever with which to fit and tension it. The traditional 'get-you-home' ploy involves using a nylon stocking to make a temporary belt; variations include using leather belts and rope; the author has thankfully not had to resort to such botch-ups – pack a spare drive belt!

BURST OIL COOLER PIPE. If you carry or can find a large enough spanner, remove the damaged pipe, undo the good pipe connection at the oil cooler radiator and fasten this to the other engine block/oil filter housing connection. Don't run the engine until you have refilled it with oil. In rural areas, most farm machinery engineers can quickly make up an oil cooler pipe using the hydraulic pipe used for tractor PTOs and the like. These are steel belt reinforced and tested to very high pressures – one of these should out-last the car!

SUMP DAMAGE. Pin holes can sometimes be dealt with using a self-tapping screw – if the damage is more severe then you'll need a replacement sump. If much oil was lost before the fault became apparent and you suspect that the bearings may have been damaged, using STP or similar can sometimes keep damaged bearing shells going for long enough to allow you to drive to a place of safety.

BROKEN SPRING LEAF. If one leaf of a spring breaks, then the side of the car concerned will drop lower than the other. This happened to the author when his car was fully laden for a holiday, and the solution was to scrounge some lengths of steel bar the same width as the spring and to affix these to the top leaf using half a dozen Jubilee clips. Crude, but it got us the 190-odd miles home!

BROKEN THROTTLE CABLE. Set the tickover to 1,500 rpm or slightly more, then change up through the gears to reach a top speed of circa 30 mph – and hope that you don't have to climb any steep hills!

BLOWING EXHAUST. Most of the sealing materials which the author has used offer strictly temporary repair – to make gums or bandage repair kits longer-lasting cover them with thin steel (from a drinks can, which can be cut with scissors) fastened with jubilee clips.

Broken Exhaust Mounting. These can usually be wired, but a jubilee clip repair will normally be longer-lasting.

SPLIT COOLANT HOSE. Waterproof (self-amalgamating) tape will usually hold the few psi of the coolant, provided that the hose exterior is cleaned off first. Hoses with large splits will have to be replaced.

BINDING BRAKES. Allow to cool. The problem could be hydraulic or mechanical – unless you can find the reason for the binding and rectify it, progress should be limited to very short hops, stopping frequently and for long periods to allow the brakes to cool fully. Best to summon a recovery service.

LEAKING RADIATOR. Proprietary repair substances are temporary measures only. Serious leaks need professional attention. Don't drive the car with no coolant.

SHATTERED WINDSCREEN. Place cloth on scuttle and bonnet to catch glass, then use heavily gloved hand or implement to push ALL shattered glass out. Open windows and quarterlights (GT) to allow air to pass through cab.

DON'T

Hot wire the ignition – you'll have no indicators for one thing, and few modern drivers recognise hand signals.

Drive with a flat tyre – it will soon come off the rim and damage both tyre and wheel – perhaps beyond repair.

Tolerate intermittent trifling electrical faults – some can suddenly become serious, permanent and terminal (both for the car and occupants).

Drive with seized brakes – fire hazard.

Live with any 'temporary' repair for a second longer than absolutely necessary.

Drive with an engine which is overheating or shows low oil pressure.

Replace a blown fuse with anything other than a fuse of the same rating – if this, too, blows, it is a warning of a short to earth which could directly cause an in-car fire.

NEVER

Drive with tyres under or over-inflated. This jeopardises roadholding, compromises handling and gives high tyre wear.

Use unleaded fuel unless the cylinder head had been specially modified.

TERMINAL FAULTS (SEND FOR THE CAVALRY)

These faults – thankfully – are all very rare, and most drivers will never suffer any of them. Should you be one of the unfortunate few, don't waste time – summon assistance at the earliest opportunity!

MECHANICAL SEIZURE. Engine – gearbox – differential.

Engine. Allow to cool fully. Don't use starter, but place in fourth gear and try to rock car backwards and forwards to see whether seizure has freed. Unless cause can be established and rectified (unlikely), don't run engine.

Gearbox/Axle/Wheel Bearing. Summon recovery service.

Broken Half Shaft. If the engine revs, the car is in gear and the speedometer indicates that the car is moving forwards – but you are going nowhere, a half shaft has broken. Summon a recovery service.

Fuel Pump Failure. Unless another pump can be fitted, summon assistance.

Appendices

Fuel   4-Star Leaded

	Gallons	Litres	US Gal.
Fuel tank (early)	10	45.4	12
(later)	12	54	14

OIL. Engine, Gearbox/overdrive, carburettor damper: SAE 20W/50 Multigrade oil

	Pint	Litre	US Pint
Engine Oil	7.5	4.26	9
+ Oil Cooler	.75	0.42	0.9
Gearbox to 18GB	4.5	2.56	5.6
18GD on	5.25	3	6
G'box/overdrive to			
18GB	5.33	3.36	6
18GD on	6	3.4	7

Automatic transmission: fluid type F

Tyre pressures
Crossply	18/19 psi	front
	18/22 psi	rear
Radial	20/21 psi	front
	24psi	rear

GENERAL CAPACITIES

	Pint	Litre	US Pint
Auto transmission	10.5	6	12.7
Rear axle 3/4 floating	2.25	1.28	2.75
Semi floating	1.5	0.85	2
Cooling system			
(early cars)	9.5	5.4	11.4
18V (GHN5 GHD5			
from 410002)	11.5	6.6	13.8
With heater			
(early cars)	10	5.68	12
18V (GHN5 GHD5			
from 410002)	12	6.8	14.4

SPARK PLUGS

	Gap
Champion N-9Y	.035"
Contact Breaker gap	.014 to .016"

Ignition timing (degrees BTDC)

		Static	Dynamic
18G	High compression	10	14
	Low compression	8	12
18V5	High compression	10	13
	Low compression	10	13
18V		5	15
18V7*		6	11
18V8*		7	10

Note: '*' denotes followed by any other numbers and letters.

RECOMMENDED LUBRICANTS AND FLUIDS

Rear axle/steering rack:
SAE 90 EP Hypoid

Grease nipples:
Lithium multi-purpose grease.

Dampers:
Armstrong thin fluid

TORQUE WRENCH SETTINGS

ENGINE

	(ft.lbs)	(kg.m)
Main bearings nuts	70	9.7
Big end bolts	35-40	4.8-5.5
Little end bolts		
(early cars)	25	3.4
Flywheel bolts	40	5.5
Clutch to flywheel bolts	25-30	3.4-4.1
Cylinder head nuts	45-50	6.2-6.9
Rocker post bolts	25	3.4
Rocker box cover nuts	4	0.56
Oil pump nuts	14	1.9
Oil pipe banjo	37	5.1
Oil release valve		
dome nut	43	5.9
Sump bolts	6	0.8
Crankshaft pulley nut	70	9.6
Camshaft nut	65	8.9
Timing cover .25" screws	6	0.8
.31" screws	14	1.9
Front plate	20	2.8
Rear plate .31" screws	20	2.8
.31" screws 18V	30	4.1
.375" screws	30	4.1
Water pump bolts	17	2.4
Manifold nuts	15	2.1
Oil filter bolt (early cars)	15	2.1
Carburettor stud		
nuts to 18V	2	0.28
18V	15	2.1
Distributor clamp bolt		
(25D4)	4.1	0.57
nut (45D4)	2.5	0.35

STEERING/SUSPENSION

	(ft.lbs)	(kg.m)
Steering arm bolts	60-65	8.3-8.9
Steering wheel		
nut 9/16" UNF	27-29	3.73-4.01
11/16" UNF	41-43	5.66-5.94
Export cars	36-38	4.98-5.26
Steering tie rod		
locknut	33-37	4.6-5.2
Steering lever ball		
joint nut	34-35	4.7-4.8
Steering column universal		
joint bolt	20-22	2.8-3
Front damper bolts	43-45	5.9-6.2
Rear damper bolts	55-60	7.6-8.3
Brake disc to hub	40-45	5.5-6.2
Brake calliper bolts	40-45	5.5-6.2
Wheel bearing nut	40-70	5.5-9.7
Crossmember to		
body	54-56	7.5-7.7

VARIOUS

Spark plugs	18	2.5
Road wheel nuts	60-65	8.3-9

SOME USEFUL ADDRESSES

The MG Owner's Club, Swavesey, Cambridge, CB4 1BR

The MG Car Club, PO Box 251 Kimber House, Cemetery Road, Abingdon, Oxon. OX14 1F

The North American MGB Register, PO Box MGB, Akin, Illinois 62805

Index